Seeds of **Freedom**

Hay House Titles of Related Interest

Seeds of Freedom

Cultivating a Life That Matters

HEATHER MARIE WILSON

HAY HOUSE, INC.
Carlsbad, California • New York City
London • Sydney • Johannesburg
Vancouver • Hong Kong • New Delhi

Published and distributed in the United States by: Hay House, Inc.: www.hayhouse .com • **Published and distributed in Australia by:** Hay House Australia Pty. Ltd.: www .hayhouse.com.au • **Published and distributed in the United Kingdom by:** Hay House UK, Ltd.: www.hayhouse.co.uk • **Published and distributed in the Republic of South Africa by:** Hay House SA (Pty), Ltd.: www.hayhouse.co.za • **Distributed in Canada by:** Raincoast: www.raincoast.com • **Published in India by:** Hay House Publishers India: www.hayhouse.co.in

Editorial supervision: Jill Kramer • *Project editor:* Patrick Gabrysiak
Cover design: Charles McStravick • *Interior design:* Tricia Breidenthal

Library of Congress Cataloging-in-Publication Data

Wilson, Heather Marie.
  Seeds of freedom : cultivating a life that matters / Heather Marie Wilson.
      p. cm.
  ISBN 978-1-4019-2903-9 (pbk. : alk. paper) 1. Self-realization. 2. Joy. 3. Quality of life.
4. Success. I. Title.
  BF637.S4W555 2011
  158.1--dc22
                                            2011014618

Tradepaper ISBN: 978-1-4019-2903-9
Digital ISBN: 978-1-4019-2904-6

14 13 12 11   4 3 2 1
1st edition, September 2011

Printed in the United States of America

This book is dedicated to my parents, who gave me the freedom and support to dig deeper; and to Summer, who taught me how to plant the Seeds of Freedom in my life so I could come into my wholeness, own my power, connect with my higher self, and be free to experience my joy.

Contents

Introduction

MY LIFE GARDEN

"Look deep into nature, and then
you will understand everything better."
— ALBERT EINSTEIN

The alarm went off. Since it had only been a few hours since I'd gone to bed, I rolled over and hit the snooze button. I dreaded opening my eyes and starting the day. I could feel the heavy burden of having to face the fire hose of responsibilities that awaited me at the office. I really enjoyed my job and was energized by the work, but it had become all-consuming at some point. My work had even crept into my dreams at night.

Before I knew it, the alarm went off again. Grabbing my Black-Berry, I squinted at my e-mail and then shuffled into the bathroom. I quickly took a shower, washed my hair, and looked at the clock. *Arrggh! Late again.* I rummaged through my clothes for something to wear, but everything in my closet was black. Black pants. Black dresses. Black shoes. Black sweaters. When did my clothes start to feel like a uniform instead of the creative self-expression of joyful colors, world-jewelry collections, and beautiful fabrics that I'd always imagined I'd wear when I was a corporate executive?

After packing my gym bag, I ran out the door with a granola bar and a small black canvas cooler containing my lunch of a Lean Cuisine and a Diet Coke. The first stop I made was to Dunkin' Donuts for my "usual." All fueled up with caffeine and carbs—just like every morning—I headed into work to face the never-ending stream of requests, e-mails, and decisions.

It was almost nine o'clock when I walked past the sea of cubicles lining the hallway leading to my office. Most of my colleagues had been there since seven or eight that morning, so their condemning stares made me feel like a slacker. No one said anything, but the looks on their faces said it all. I wanted to tell them that I'd worked until ten the night before, but I didn't. Instead, I just tried to give them a smile as I made my way down the hall to my office. Once there, I rolled up my sleeves to attack the mountain of work that had landed on my desk in the few short hours I'd been away.

Work always came first, and the long list of "emergencies" I tended to face in the course of my day routinely caused me to put myself last. For example, on this particular day, my boss asked me to join him for an impromptu meeting—and since I was eager to please, I attended. After all, I was a good corporate citizen playing my role within the company culture. Going to the gym seemed indulgent, and the possibility of getting there grew more and more distant even though the company touted the benefits of a wellness program. By the time the meeting ended, the gym was closed, and my body was out of energy. I went home, ate a quick dinner, and went to bed so that I could get up the next day and do the whole thing all over again.

As each day went by, I felt more and more like a hamster on an exercise wheel. I was running on empty. I had dreamed of living a creative and meaningful life, but the reality was that there was no time for anything but work, work, and more work. There was no time for friends or hiking or that salsa class I'd always wanted to take. There was no time to build a relationship with a partner, learn a new language, or travel to exotic places. How had I gotten here? I'd always been a vivacious and exciting woman who wanted to live life to the fullest, yet now I felt as if I were living in a prison. It was a prison of conformity, and I didn't fit in.

Then one day I stared out my office window and noticed a scattering of violets among the grass. They reminded me of the wild violets where I'd grown up, but unlike those of my youth, I was unable to reach these flowers that were growing outside. It dawned on me that all of my accomplishments—my external success—meant nothing if I wasn't interacting in the world. I realized that I was trapped behind glass like an animal in the zoo. I was inside an office building for most hours of the day with fluorescent lights instead of sunshine, artificial plants instead of real ones, and circulated air instead of fresh. Was my entire life artificial as well?

All of a sudden, I had a flash of knowing and realized that the prison bars were in my mind. I was responsible for creating my own happiness, and I'd allowed my life to be gobbled up by my professional responsibilities at the expense of practically everything else. No wonder I was miserable! And the worst part was that I was the one who had imprisoned myself. But if I were my own jailer, then I also had the power to set myself free. The trouble was, I wasn't quite sure how to go about changing my life. I felt that I had so much to lose: a big job, a big salary, and a big house (with a great big mortgage). I didn't want to free myself from a work prison only to hurl myself into one of financial anxiety. I didn't know quite what to do, but one thing was clear: I had to do something. I couldn't continue living my life as I had been. It was time to break free!

So I decided to plant a garden. This is not as much of a non sequitur as it might sound. I grew up around my parents' garden center, and I come from a long line of farmers and gardeners. My maternal grandparents, immigrants from Finland and Sweden, were both raised on farms, and they had brought their skills to America. Consequently, they were able to support their family by growing fresh fruits and vegetables, raising chickens for eggs and meat, and also keeping a cow or two for milk and butter.

During the 1940s, people who had land grew "victory gardens" to reduce the pressure of the public food supply (they also raised animals because there was a scarcity of butter and other farm products).

Since many individuals didn't have fresh vegetables and meat at this time, my grandmother was able to supplement the family income by selling whatever extra she had from the garden. She was also especially skilled in the kitchen and was able to make fresh and delicious meals from what she grew on the farm, and knew how to preserve and store items to get her family members through the long New England winter months with full bellies and smiles on their faces. My grandfather was a home builder and could fix or repair anything around the house or on the farm. It truly was a self-sufficient, connected, harmonious, and happy home.

My paternal grandfather—or "Papa," as all of the grandkids called him—also grew up with farming in his blood. He always had a full and bountiful garden on the side of his home, and he saved seeds in old coffee cans and mason jars in the basement right next to all the trinkets and doodads that you tend to find in a grandfather's basement. I remember him bringing us these large brown shopping bags each weekend filled with a selection of peppers, tomatoes, squash, and cucumbers.

It was Papa's love of gardening that encouraged my dad to start working on the nearby farms when he was just a boy. That early exposure eventually led him to a job at the University of Massachusetts Extension helping the various communities across Massachusetts with their horticultural questions and needs. Fortunately, the scientists that worked with my dad recognized his potential and urged him to study both business and horticulture at the University of Massachusetts, Amherst (my alma mater as well). He was the first person in his family to get a college degree.

When my mother and father met, they were 22 and 27 years old, respectively. They used most of their savings to purchase a garden center and a nursery surrounded by acres of fertile farmland in a small community about an hour south of Boston. It was an idyllic landscape that was thick with verdant woods, streams teeming with tadpoles, and black-and-white cows grazing peacefully in pastures strewn with wildflowers. My dad became a local celebrity as the "Garden Doctor" on the nearby radio station, where he took questions from

callers about their ailing plants, bug-infested shrubs, or any other horticultural concerns that plagued those who listened to the show.

Naturally, he also taught my sister and me how to plant our own
garden every year. We had watermelon, zucchini, peppers, tomatoes,
summer squash, string beans, cucumbers, and lettuce. I can still visualize the placement of most of those plants in that first garden.
During those summers in the vegetable garden, I learned some of
the most important lessons of my life. I understood that if you plant a
watermelon seed and give it the right nourishment, care, and protection, you actually get to enjoy a beautiful red and ripe watermelon in
late summer. That seemed miraculous to me as a child.

My mother had always wanted a place in the country where we
kids would have the freedom to play in the woods and learn about
nature. Even more important to her than this, though, was the desire
to run her own business alongside my dad. Over the years, Bel-Air
Gardens became a beautiful and successful garden center and nursery. Running this business in a small town wasn't always an easy life,
but my parents had a sense of freedom, were happy with each other
and in their work, and were in control of their own destiny. So what
had happened to their daughter?

That day in my office when I saw those beautiful and fragile violets basking in the sun, I suddenly realized the problem: I had forgotten some really simple but important truths from my childhood.

Even though I was now an adult, I'd somehow surrendered control over my own destiny. I'd traded my freedom for the security of
a high-paying job in corporate America, a nice house, and a healthy
401(k) plan. I'd unknowingly followed the crowd on a path to a destination that I'd never envisioned. I'd lost track of who I was, what
I wanted, and what made me happy—and I now felt the so-called
secure foundation I had created crumbling under my feet. I'd made
a bad deal because I'd sacrificed my soul, my spirit, and my sense of
joyful and creative expression in exchange for things that didn't matter. I had to bring my life back into balance and regain control over

my own destiny, my own happiness, and my own internal sense of security.

So I planted a garden. I thought that if the power of the Universe made that tender little violet so beautiful and strong, maybe planting a garden would not only get me back to my roots, but also help me tap into that power of the Universe to find myself. If nothing else, I thought it would help me focus on something that was alive and growing. I wanted to plunge my hands into the coolness of the dirt, feel the warmth of the sunshine on my face, and stir up the creative juices that used to flow so freely within me.

I thought it would be fun to plant a few seeds in the earth and wait to see what emerged. I was sure it would help me cultivate a new way of being, as well as remind me of something I used to know when I was eight years old—that watermelons, peas, bees, butterflies, and violets are nothing short of miracles. After all, we're all a part of this incredible Universe, and expressing the uniqueness of our soul matters in the world.

At this time, I was living on the outskirts of Atlanta, Georgia, in a townhome surrounded by trees and lush ground cover. I realized that a small clearing behind my house and both the front and back decks could be used for my gardening adventure. I started out small and planted loads of herbs such as basil, cilantro, parsley, oregano, and rosemary; as well as some basic vegetables like tomatoes, lettuce, and string beans. The items I selected were mostly practical ones that I could eat or use in my everyday cooking. I did, however, buy a special violet that I placed by my bedside as a reminder of my connection to the aliveness of the world. My life was starting to shift from being totally artificial to having some life in it.

In the beginning, I thought of my garden as a flicker of light in the vast darkness. But the more time I spent with my plants, the brighter the light became . . . and I realized that I was moving toward something magnificent. I was discovering freedom. Planting that garden actually saved my life.

The lessons I learned about being present in the moment—about the importance of the elemental gifts of nourishment and connection, light and shade, balance and renewal—sowed the seeds of freedom, greater meaning, and peaceful happiness that eventually bloomed throughout my whole life. But at the time, I had no idea how important this small exercise would become.

◎

At one point or another, I think everyone is confronted by a fundamental choice: to either play it safe and continue living as they have, or to rely on faith and find the courage to confront the unknown and discover new things and a better way of being. I didn't know that I was making this choice when I first committed to a garden. I didn't see it as a courageous choice. I had no idea that this exercise would become life altering. I didn't know I had just stepped on to the freedom path. But that's exactly what happened. It didn't require any huge tectonic shifts in my circumstances, although it did eventually lead to that. All it took was paying attention to the lessons I learned in my garden and then applying them to my life.

Whenever any of us plants new seeds, they start out as dreams—but when we nourish those seeds with our attention and love, what we get are the blossoms of our life. It was in the garden that I learned to see the fertile ground of possibilities and plant the Seeds of Freedom. Of course, the fruits of my labor didn't appear overnight. Sometimes it felt as if nothing would ever spring up through the barren soil, let alone produce fruit or flowers. During those times, however, I learned to appreciate small miracles such as a new bud or a fresh green shoot, which were nature's way of reassuring me. Today, as I take in the beauty and abundance in my garden, it reflects back to me the essence of my truth, aspirations, core beliefs, and joy.

Planting a garden helps us be alone with our thoughts, connect with ourselves, find our peace, and understand our place in the world. We all matter when we plant a garden, and we *know* that we matter. The garden raises our consciousness and integrates us with the world around us. In the garden, a violet is just a violet—ever present and beautiful—and that's all it has to worry about doing or being. It doesn't try to be a rose or an orchid. It just does the best job it can at being a violet and relies on support from the Universe, and sometimes the gardener, to provide what it needs in order to flourish. We can all learn a lot from those sweet little violets. I know I did.

As I cared for my plants and provided all of the essentials they needed to survive in their environment, I began to realize that I had to learn to care for myself in the very same way. I also needed water, food, fresh air, rest, and a connection to the Universe in order to thrive. So I started making sure that I got enough sleep, healthy food, and exercise; I also took the time to be silent and connect to something greater than I was. And sure enough, I, like the violet, began to put out new shoots and even a few buds. I began to feel a renewed belief in my connection to the Universe, and things soon started to grow in my life as if by magic.

What I Learned

Caring for my garden taught me so many things. I learned how I fit in the world, and about the cycle of death and renewal. I learned to pay more attention to the wonder in my life, and to achieve a greater sense of joy and fulfillment. Growing a garden helped me come back to myself. By meticulously cultivating each of my plants, I learned about love and commitment, as well as how to trust and believe in myself. My garden helped me understand that I can rely on my connection to the power of the Universe, no matter the weather. Through the garden, I now know with certainty, like the violet does, that I am enough, just as I am.

As I planted my string beans, basil, and begonias, I learned a lot about what makes a garden grow. But at the same time, I was also planting a garden in my heart. As I embarked on a journey to self, I realized how the lessons I was learning in my garden were applicable to my life as well. So I started applying those lessons to what I termed my "Life Garden." Note that I'll be using the term *Life Garden* throughout the book to explain how *you* can use the principles I learned in the garden to create an abundant and flourishing life for yourself.

Words don't teach. It's only life experience that instructs and transforms us. It doesn't matter how much we study, how many seminars we take, or how many books we read—all those things are outside of us. It's our personal experience that is always the best teacher. So, as I started applying the lessons from my vegetable garden to my Life Garden, I began to understand the multidimensionality of my life. When I looked at it as organic, alive, evolving, and multidimensional—instead of static, dead, arrived, and one-dimensional—then it could expand to new possibilities.

As I watched my life transform, I decided to write down the lessons I'd learned and came up with the nine Seeds of Freedom that I planted in my Life Garden, from which I have reaped a harvest that has changed my entire life. They are: *Exploration, Focus, Rooting, Nourishment, Growth, Connection, Balance, Clearing,* and *Renewal*.

I began to share the principles of this framework with friends, clients, organizations, and businesses, and people got it. But when I combined the power of this framework with what I learned in the garden, I started to see men and women totally transform their lives by planting those seeds—real or metaphorical.

Caring for a plant can be the start of an incredible journey inward. I want to share this with you because when you find such a source of freedom, such a source of joy, and have had such a transformational experience that you didn't even know existed, you want everyone to feel as good as you do.

Although planting a garden absolutely saved my life, of course my life is far from perfect. I still have challenges, frustrations, and anxieties. But I also have a deep knowing that I'm headed in the right direction, and I'm finding joy in the journey, no matter where it leads. Now I can look at an unfavorable situation and say *thank you,* and then move through and beyond it. It's pretty powerful to know that nothing can knock me down, because I'll always know that I am enough just as I am. We all want to be accepted just as we are. I am now experiencing a trust, a peace, a love, and a knowing like I've never experienced before. I am, like a garden in springtime, renewed.

Your Life Garden

Do you ever think, *Is this it? Is this all there is? There's got to be more to life than this!* Is your life starting to feel like a series of tasks that you either pass or fail? School, *pass;* career, *pass;* home, *pass;* marriage, *fail;* kids, *pass;* health, *fail;* investments, *fail;* friends, *pass.* Up until this point, you've probably been able to attain almost everything you've ever set your mind to—job, home, relationship, friends, social life, or other personal achievements—but now it feels as if there's something missing. Maybe you've dreamed of running away and starting over, or it could be that you don't know what to do next and that's a frightening thought. Maybe you yearn for deeper experiences of love, intimacy, and connection. Or perhaps you want to feel more fully alive and present in your life, or that you're serving a purpose larger than yourself.

If you're reading this book, then you're seeking freedom from something or looking for more purpose in your life, and you must believe that there is more to it than your current circumstances. What you've been doing isn't working anymore. Well, whatever you're dealing with, know that I wrote this book to assure you that you're not alone. And you're not stuck—you can find freedom, just like I did, as soon as you're ready to plant the Seeds of Freedom in your Life Garden and make the shift from living a life driven by external success to cultivating one that's nourished by the treasures within you.

We all possess the power to create, nurture, and transform our lives so that we can have a joy-filled life on our own terms. No one can grant us freedom, and no one can take it away from us. We were all born to be free: free to love; free to speak our own truth; free to express ourselves; and free to live life with an unshakable sense of security, abundance, and vitality.

Freedom is a state of being—and by doing this work, you'll not only become more liberated, but you'll also become more self-aware, conscious, and engaged. When you decide to plant the Seeds of Freedom, then you'll be embarking on a deep and spiritual journey inward to know that you matter.

I want to share the Seeds of Freedom with you so you can experience the benefit of uncovering your own truths, aspirations, and gifts; and so you can be true to yourself instead of listening to what others tell you. You'll learn to challenge the status quo—and even some of your own beliefs—and redefine success.

Now, living life on your own terms takes courage, commitment, and consistency. Just like planting a garden, it's hard work. But the good news is that you already have all of the seeds you need to build a happier, freer, and more fulfilling life. All you have to do is plant them in your life and then tend to them.

Any gardener will tell you that growing a garden doesn't happen overnight, but rather it's an incredible and magical journey. A garden teaches that you reap what you sow. So what are you sowing in your Life Garden? Are you cultivating your inner growth and knowledge of self? Or are you cultivating anxiety, exhaustion, depletion, and self-doubt? If so, then perhaps it's time to take back some control and reap a harvest that brings you true joy and fulfillment.

As you start to plant the nine seeds in your Life Garden, you'll find that it's not about making anything happen, but about co-creating what you want with the Universe. You must explore your own needs and desires; focus on your vision; root in your new beliefs; nourish yourself with love; grow and connect with the power of your heart; and then balance, clear, and renew your garden every day. If you do this, then you will flourish with joy, abundance, and freedom.

Please keep in mind that each seed is something you plant and continue to cultivate for the rest of your life. It's not something you do and then forget about. When you plant the Seeds of Freedom, you're integrating these concepts into your life so that you'll be able to experience the love, peace, truth, clarity, vitality, courage, and possibilities of your existence forever.

The promise of a flower is within every seed, just as the promise to lead a wonderful life is within each of us. We are living in an extraordinary, leading-edge time of rising consciousness, and an opening up of healing and growth. If there is any time to plant your garden, it's now. The purpose of this book is to help you create a purposeful and authentic life aligned with your highest self. It will teach you how to grow your own Life Garden so that you're able to handle any storms or seasons. In the Life Garden, the definition of *success* isn't based on money, fame, or accomplishments; it's based on each individual plant doing its best with what it's given.

Your journey will be uniquely yours, so this book is not prescriptive or linear. You get to choose your own path and create your own garden . . . and if you're ready to take responsibility for your life, dedicate the time to do the work, and fully embrace life, then the destination will be the same. Be easy on yourself. It took you an entire lifetime to get where you are today, so don't expect everything to change in an instant. You *will* experience your own Life Garden, a place where your existence in the world matters—a place where you can tune in to the invisible messages and spirit of nature, share your gifts with the world, and just be you.

How to Use This Book

This book is not something to be quickly consumed and tossed aside. Rather, if you're serious about planting the Seeds of Freedom in your life, then I encourage you to read slowly and commit to the practices. There are written exercises throughout the chapters that will require you to have a journal or notebook handy. In my experience, I find that it's good to select a journal you love, which can be designated specifically for these exercises so that you accumulate the energy of your transformation in one place.

To make lasting changes in your life, you must be willing to do the inner work necessary for transformation. If you're looking to fully experience the wonder of life, then you will need to release any pain from your past. It's not always easy to work with these energies, as they can be so suppressed that you're not even aware of them. However, if you take full responsibility for your life and commit to doing the inner work, you'll be able to move through any feelings and emotions that you've been holding in your body.

As you dig deeper into your life, you'll start to connect with the essence of your real self, or your higher self. Over the course of this book, I'll be discussing the intelligence of nature and spirit. I use the terms *Universe, higher power, energy, source energy, spirit, consciousness,* and *higher self* interchangeably; you can also use *God, Holy Spirit, Allah,* or *the Almighty* in place of the words that I use. Whatever you choose to call it, *Seeds of Freedom* will help you tap into the divine energy or spirit of the Universe so that you can live your life in alignment with an intelligence and power far greater than you can conceive.

For the sake of this book, I had to collapse a multidimensional framework into a linear process using one concept per chapter, but the ideas and exercises in each chapter are not dependent on the previous chapters. You can pick and choose which seeds you want to plant in your garden first, but only when you've planted all the seeds in your life will your real garden and your Life Garden be able to thrive and flourish.

The lessons detailed in these pages were written for you as an individual and can be applied to all aspects of your life. Yet the book has been created so that you can also share the principles of your personal transformation with your family members, your teams, your organizations, or your businesses to create a more fulfilling and long-lasting definition of success. I believe that personal transformation leads to lasting and positive transformation in your home, your community, your social structures, and your workplace. To that end, I've also included stories from people I've met along my path to freedom. (Some names and details have been omitted or changed to protect personal identities, but the essence of the stories is the same.) I'm confident that these associates, clients, and friends of mine will inspire you and show you how different types of people have created lives that matter.

In each chapter, I offer you all of the instructions you'll need to plant, cultivate, and nurture each of the nine Seeds of Freedom. And you can do the work anywhere. You can create a "freedom garden" at home, in your community, or even in your workplace. This book is designed to help you create an internal place where you can relax into the flow of life, feel the energy of everything around you, and allow the spirit of nature to help you grow into your best self. It's not about doing more or being good enough; it's about being you. It's about genuinely connecting with self, knowing what is right for you, listening to energy, and finding joy in the present moment.

Freedom not only means that we're empowered, independent, and self-sufficient, but also that we're secure in our place in the world, full of vitality, loving to self and to others, doing work that matters, and tapping into our highest creative expressions. Freedom will elevate you, challenge you, and transform you to new heights and new dimensions that you didn't know existed.

Once you start to experience a life of freedom—a life that is true to who you really are, which you are living on your own terms—you'll be amazed by how good you start to feel, as well as how quickly your Garden grows. So, if you're feeling lost, stuck, or just plain fed up with the rat race and wondering about the meaning of it all, I invite you to plant the nine Seeds of Freedom in your Life Garden. You'll be delighted by what grows and blossoms.

If you're ready to start cultivating your Life Garden and create a life that matters, then let's get started!

EXPLORATION

"The real voyage of discovery consists not in seeking
new landscapes but in having new eyes."

— MARCEL PROUST

Before I ever put a seed into the earth, I decided that I would
explore beautiful gardens in my area and reacquaint myself with the
different styles, what other people were doing, what resources were
available, and what I might like to plant.

As I was now living in Atlanta, Georgia, my journey of exploration
began in the most obvious places, such as the local nurseries, the gardening section of Barnes & Noble, and my friends' backyards; along
with more formal settings like the Atlanta Botanical Garden and the
rose garden at the Jimmy Carter Library & Museum. My family was
also a big help in offering guidance and support. Basically, I spent a
lot of time just looking around and observing the various elements
that went into each type of garden, and I also paid attention to the
way they all made me *feel.*

One of the very first things I noticed was that although my interest in gardens was new, my exploration was uncovering some

old memories. It was putting me in touch with some fundamental parts of my younger self that I'd forgotten as soon as I'd grown up and gotten a real job, and the hectic routine of life had taken over. I began to remember what I'd enjoyed about gardening as a child. I recalled what kinds of plants I'd liked looking at, what fresh fruits and veggies I'd preferred to eat, and what my favorite flowers had been. I also remembered something completely unrelated to gardens: my love of sailing.

Many of my childhood summers were spent at our family cottage at Alexander Lake in northeast Connecticut. I relished being at that cottage: I spent day after happy day swimming in the lake, riding my bike through the forest, roller-skating at the old pavilion, catching fish off the dock, or riding horses through the cornfields. At night I caught fireflies in old mayonnaise or pickle jars, and when it rained, I played *Monopoly* with my family. All of these were great pastimes . . . but what I enjoyed most of all about those summers was sailing.

Sailing was something I connected with the moment I saw my very first sailboat. No one in my family sailed, nor did I take lessons or have a friend who could show me the ropes. For some reason, though, I just knew that I loved sailing. I loved everything about it. I remember the feeling of extreme joy as I skimmed across the top of the water with just the sound of the ducks quacking in the coves, or watching the colorful triangles of red and white or the rainbow-colored spinnakers race by the cottage on Sunday mornings. I dreamed of one day being able to buy my own boat and becoming a real sailor.

In our youth, we feel free to reach out and make things that inspired us as children a part of our lives, and that is exactly what I did with sailing. Even though I didn't have a boat of my own, I injected sailing into my life as much as I was able. I went out on the water with friends, bought sailing-related items, and took a few lessons. I enjoyed sailing in some of the most beautiful places in the world, such as Newport, Rhode Island; New York Harbor; the Hawaiian Islands; the British Virgin Islands; and Catalina Island, which is located off the coast of California.

As I rediscovered my passion for sailing, I realized that as I'd gotten older, I'd felt less and less free to reach out and enjoy the things

I loved. I was working all the time or too busy with things around the house, and I seemed to be forever punching out a never-ending to-do list. What was so easy to recognize as a child—the activities that filled me with energy and joy, as well as how to fearlessly include those things in my life—had escaped me. And eventually, I'd completely forgotten what had so captivated my imagination when I was younger.

So one of the seeds of exploration I planted was to reacquaint myself with the world of sailing. I signed up for a weeklong, live-aboard class in my old stomping ground of Newport to see if I could remember what I had loved so much about this experience in my early years. I had gone to high school in Rhode Island and had spent many summer days visiting the beaches, restaurants, and shops of Newport. It was one of my favorite places to be in the world.

On a gorgeous Tuesday morning in the middle of July, my fellow sailors and I boarded a 43-foot Dufour sailboat named *Weatherbird*. As we came out of Newport Harbor, we passed the many famous yacht clubs, stately mansions, sturdy old lighthouses, and 19th-century military forts built along the seashore of the "sailing capital of the world." It was the first time I'd viewed the stunning landscapes of Newport and Jamestown from a sailboat gliding across the water instead of from the safety of the Rhode Island shores. I reveled in the thought that I was actually going to be living on the *Weatherbird* for a week.

As we navigated the waters of Newport and the surrounding islands, Captain Joe and the three other sailing students didn't realize that I was exploring more than the Atlantic. I was on a journey to explore my inner self and rediscover the joy I wanted to plant in my new Life Garden.

The Power of Exploration

Taking action—such as following up on a forgotten desire, even if it feels out of reach—helps us figure out what we really want in life. Sometimes we think we want something and we turn out to be wrong. Then again, we may turn out to be very right, and discover a passion that illuminates and gives shape to the rest of our lives. When we make the decision to explore, we learn more about our own desires and eventually free up the mental and physical energy we need in order to cultivate what we truly value. This is as true for a sailing trip as it is for dealing with a difficult relationship or even cleaning out the garage. When we explore what we want, we're discovering what we'd like to keep in our Life Gardens, and what we want to weed out.

Exploration is a powerful process of self-discovery. It's about investigating the world around us and finding out what brings us joy and what brings us frustration. Through a process of exploration, we find out what we like, what we *don't* like, and what is missing in our lives. Clearly, I'd been missing out on sailing . . . but I discovered that I'd been missing out on some other things, too. My love of adventure, for example, which had once ignited my passion for living on so many levels, had completely disappeared.

After college, I had the opportunity to teach English in Hawaii and Japan, and I was able to travel through much of Southeast Asia as well. It was a heady experience, to be sure—I met new and interesting people from all over the world and visited places I never even dreamed existed. While my peers were starting their first jobs and spending the weekends at the local pub or dance club, I was riding elephants in Chiang Mai, wandering the streets of Hong Kong, and soaking in Japanese hot springs. It was a magical time of adventure, discovery, and trying new things.

As time went on, I realized that I was missing out on a lot of important events, such as friends' weddings, family gatherings, and establishing a life for myself. So I headed back to the East Coast to get a job, and landed in Atlanta. I quickly settled into working long hours trying to "get ahead," enrolled in business school, and ascended the corporate ladder—my definition of success at that time. Those years were a whirlwind. Looking back now, I see that my life was consumed by long hours and lots of sacrifice.

I lost track of what I liked and what I didn't. My existence had become a series of tasks and to-do lists, as well as the next thing I needed to accumulate to round out my "success portfolio." It didn't matter if it was a material possession, a piece of real estate, an exciting new project at work, or a promotion, I thought I was headed in the direction of success and had the assets to prove it.

My Life Garden—which had once been full of adventure, exotic locations, interesting people, and fulfilling experiences—had become a barren patch of "same old, same old." I was bored, living alone in a landlocked city, and totally stressed-out. As I looked around, I realized that this Garden didn't represent who I was and what I loved, but I felt trapped and unable to make any kind of change.

What really paralyzed me is that I didn't know what I truly wanted. My path hadn't led to the idyllic destination of marriage and family life I had always imagined. I thought those were my life goals, but they hadn't panned out yet. I thought I wanted to have a home to entertain friends, but I rarely made time to have anyone over. I thought I wanted to travel more, but my vacation time was limited to three weeks per year and was used up mostly by short trips and holidays. The life I'd envisioned for myself was so different from what I'd actually created . . . but I should have been happy, right? I had a good job, a beautiful home, a pretty comfortable life, and my health. I was living the American Dream, wasn't I? So what was the problem?

Then one day I became so upset by some things that happened at work that I broke down in front of my friend and colleague Paula, who was one of the sweetest, most balanced people in my life. She looked at me with great compassion and said, "Heather, you're not going to find what you're looking for here."

I don't know why that statement seemed so profound at that moment, or why something so obvious to me now wasn't then. But this is where my exploration led me: to a discovery that my job was making me miserable. I was going to have to take a long, hard look at the Life Garden I'd created and make some changes . . . or I wasn't going to survive.

Exploring the Five Elements of Your Life Garden

No matter who we are, our Life Gardens are made up of the same basic elements that we find in nature: *earth,* which gives us security;

water, which brings us health and well-being; *fire,* which fuels our passion for our vocation or calling in life; *air,* which provides the necessary breath in our relationships; and *spirit,* which feeds our creative expression. All living beings are formed out of these same elements, and the proper balance of each of them is critical to our overall happiness.

As you look at all five elements in your current Life Garden, it would be helpful to thoroughly examine each one by answering the following questions (write down your answers in your journal or notebook). Be as honest as possible about what you see, how you feel, and what you like or don't like because you're going to use the answers to these questions to create your ideal Life Garden vision later in the chapter.

1. *Earth:* Security

The earth is tied to our sense of security because it shelters and supports our roots. When our roots are deep and protected by the earth, they're able to bring us all of the nutrients we need to survive. And thanks to the reliable source of food and water that the earth provides, we're free to enjoy a vibrant and sustainable quality of life. With our root system in place, we're able to grow stronger and create bigger blooms that can weather the storms of life. When we're securely grounded, we then have the freedom and security to live from a place of comfort, ease, and confidence.

Security doesn't just come from having a marriage certificate, a healthy bank account, or a job with an established company. Security comes from knowing that you have the strength and courage to live an authentic life—that you'll be nourished and sustained, come what may. Having strong roots means that you can trust and believe that you will always be cared for and have what you need to survive, because the earth will give it to you.

My personal exploration had revealed that I was unhappy in my job, but I didn't have the sense of security necessary to make much of a change in my life right away. My beliefs about title, success, and money; my actual financial situation; and my grounding in the earth wasn't stable enough yet for me to create the kind of Life Garden I was envisioning.

As I started to further explore the idea of quitting my job by talking to other people about it, making different financial decisions, and actually visualizing what might happen if I made the leap, I got more comfortable with the idea.

One exercise that was powerful for me at the beginning of my exploration was to ask myself, *What's the worst thing that could happen?* Then I allowed myself to explore every worst-case scenario I could imagine. Whatever I envisioned, I ultimately realized that I had family and friends who would be there for me no matter what—they'd even take me in and feed me if necessary. It would be a humbling experience, sure, but I knew that I wouldn't change as a human being if all my possessions, titles, and measures of external success changed. And I knew that Mother Earth would provide for me. It was a powerful moment.

It was this visualization exercise alone that gave me the courage to make one of the most significant decisions in my life and leave my reliable job as a corporate executive. My security came not from a steady paycheck, a fabulous house, or the ability to buy dinner at a nice restaurant, but from the knowledge that I would always be okay no matter how much money I had or did not have at any given moment.

If *you* are currently living in a place of fear, insecurity, or worry, then you need to take a look at the earth element in your garden. What kind of ground are you rooted in? And what can you do to make that ground more productive and secure? Here are some questions to ask yourself as you take a tour of this section of your present Life Garden:

- If you're living from a place of fear or insecurity, why is that? What are you so afraid of? What is your biggest fear?

- Are the basics in your life secure—your safety, shelter, food, water, clothing, transportation, health care, and other basic necessities? Do you have the ability to obtain these items in times of crisis?

- How stable to you feel in your life? Describe what stability looks like in your life? Do you make choices that bring more of it to your life?

- Do you have enough money to live your life comfortably? How much do you have? Do you worry about it? What are your beliefs about money?

- Do you allow yourself to dream about how you really want to live? Do you believe that what you desire can actually manifest?

- Do you own or rent your home? Describe in detail where you live—the location, type of home, environment, neighborhood, and level of safety.

- Describe your lifestyle? What kinds of things do you do in a normal day? How would you describe your quality of life? How is your life easy? How is your life difficult? Are you living the way you desire?

- How much money do you have coming in on a regular basis? Describe where it comes from? What do you do with it: How do you spend it? How do you save it? How do you give it away? Are you finances in order? Who manages your money?

- Describe what you would do differently if you knew you'd have inner peace no matter what your external circumstances were? Do you believe that you can retain your internal sense of security no matter what's happening externally? Are you able to handle change easily?

- How are you connected to nature? Do you go outdoors regularly? Describe what you love about nature? Are you aware of how you treat life on Earth?

- Do you have the courage and strength to withstand change and adversity? Describe ways in which you could be more patient.

- Can you wait for your dreams to unfold naturally? Are you appreciative of what you already have in your life?

- Are you fearful of the unknown? Do you fear going outside of your comfort level of what you know in life? Are you rooted in something greater than yourself? Do you believe that you will be protected and guided by a higher power?

When we don't have a reliable root system, we don't have the courage to make the changes necessary to nourish our seeds of potential and live our best life. And when we aren't secure, it constricts our energy—we tend not to be generous, open, and courageous because we're worried about our safety and survival, the basics of paying the bills, or figuring out how to put gas in the car or finding a place to live. When we feel secure, we can then start to move toward creating a happy and fulfilling life. It's not just about money and possessions—it's about the freedom we desire.

2. *Water:* Health and Well-being

The water in our Life Garden is not only essential to life and growth, but it has the ability to transform as well. Water's qualities include fluidity, energy, stillness, and motion. It can be smooth or rough. It's a natural, sensual, ever-changing, and creative element. The water section of our Garden is related to emotional connections;

movement; and the health of our physical, intellectual, and emotional selves.

As I considered the health and well-being area of my own Life Garden, I realized that I was often running on empty: I didn't eat right, get the rest I needed, or take the time to pamper myself in any way. I was overweight, overworked, under stress, and unhappy. So I began to focus on my health. I went to Weight Watchers, worked with a counselor to help me take control of my diet, and hit the gym on a regular basis. I made sure to drink enough water, get enough rest, and manage my stress and energy levels in healthier ways than beating the 4 o'clock slump with a Snickers bar.

I ultimately shed more than 40 pounds and increased my physical fitness by running half marathons—but I also improved my emotional and intellectual strength. I could see my options more clearly and make better and more vital decisions. I also had the energy to reach for my highest aspirations, rather than just settling for whatever came my way in life. By changing how I thought of myself internally, I had managed to make a huge shift in what was going on externally. And you can, too.

Here are some questions to ask yourself as you explore the water element in your present Life Garden:

- Are you healthy and full of vitality? Describe how you feel in your body? Do you like how you look? Do you think you could feel more alive in your current body? What would you have to change in order to support your wellness?

- How long do you think you will live? Are you afraid of getting sick or not being well?

- Do you honor your physical body by giving it enough water, food, movement, love, vitamins, and exercise?

Describe what you do in each area. Are you overweight? Stressed out? Undernourished? Out of shape?

- How healthy do you feel? Describe what health and well-being look like for you. Do you make choices that bring these things into your life?

- Do you have ailments that you suffer from repeatedly (such as headaches, neck aches, ulcers, or skin problems), or do you get sick a lot? What kind of medicines do you take? What are your beliefs about illness and drugs?

- Do you allow yourself to dream about how you really want to live? Do you believe that what you desire can actually manifest?

- Do you give yourself time to rest and just be present? Do accept your need for pleasure and create enough time and experiences to restore and replenish your mind, body, and spirit? How much time do you set aside for leisurely activities each day, and what do you do?

- Do you know how to protect your energy from people, places, and things that are toxic and draining? What kinds of things do you do to protect or enrich your energy? Do you take naps, walk in nature, turn off electronics, go for runs, go to bed early, or take baths?

- Do you acknowledge your sexuality? Do you know what you value around your sexual identity and needs? Do you believe that you deserve to enjoy pleasurable activities?

- Are you emotionally healthy? Describe your relationships with everyone in your life? How do you feel about those relationships? Do you have any secrets or built-up emotions that you haven't discussed or released?

- Do you believe that you matter in the world? Do you like who you are? How do other people see you?

- What would you do if you knew that you would have vibrant health and well-being no matter what you did? What would you do with your life if you knew you only had six months to live?

- Are you intellectually engaged and always learning new things? Do you have the education that you want? What are you doing in order to better your life?

When we have vitality and energy, we have the mental and physical strength to survive changes in our life. When we aren't healthy, we can't have a full life. It's not just about looking good—it's about feeling good in all areas of our mind, body, and spirit.

3. *Fire:* Vocation

The fire element focuses on the very foundation of who you are and what your role is in the world—it's your path in life and how you deal with your inner passions. Your vocation is fueled by your internal flame and is often described as your "life's work." It can also be called your art, business, calling, career, craft, field, or mission. When you tap into your true purpose in life, you gain a sense of self-confidence, harmony, and joy in your work. Your vocation fuels your sense of freedom. When you haven't tapped into your true purpose, you feel frustrated, bored, and even trapped. It doesn't matter if you're a CEO, an administrative assistant, a cashier, or an actor. If you love what you do, your Life Garden will flourish; if you don't, every area of it will suffer.

Fire in itself is not intrinsically good or bad—it's how we use it that determines whether it will have a negative or positive effect on our Gardens. Fire, sourced from the sun, can be used to make a meal, create glass, sterilize equipment, or warm a house. Burning a field to the ground can actually be something that is beneficial to the cycle of life, as the charred remains add nitrogen-rich fertilizer to the soil, creating a more nourishing environment. But fire can also be used to destroy and devastate everything in its path.

When I decided I wanted to leave my corporate job, I had no idea what I wanted to do instead. I knew I was smart, had good business acumen, and could do a lot of jobs well, but I had no idea what truly inspired me. My fire element was a blank slate—I could be, do, or have anything I wanted. This was actually an overwhelming proposition for a while. I thought there were too many choices in my life. How would I decide what I wanted to do? What if I made the wrong choice? What if I didn't make enough money? Did I want to be famous? Did I have to be successful right from the beginning? And what did *success* mean anyway? After all, I'd already achieved it at one vocation, and it was making me miserable.

As I kept exploring, I realized that I'd always felt a lot of pressure to be successful—to do something magnificent, make a lot of money, or become somebody special. Once I realized that I was enough just as I was, the pressure lifted, and I felt free to begin exploring different kinds of work. Being the best or the biggest wasn't important anymore; I just had to be me. But who was that?

I mentally explored a lot of different potential directions for myself. I thought about starting a coaching service, a consulting firm, a staffing agency, a travel business, a T-shirt company, a dating service, a real-estate-renovation business, a speakers' bureau, a video company, a publishing house, a magazine, and a few more that I've forgotten now. Then I went about the exploration of the fire in my Life Garden from a business perspective and learned as much as I could about each option under consideration. This type of exploration was extremely helpful for me because I got to know players in the industry, mapped out the process of work, and actually put together a business plan for each of my ideas. It was very practical and strategic, but even as I was going through this left-brained process, I was learning a lot of things. And I was imagining alternatives for myself that would ultimately lead to a better life.

This process of elimination was a time of great freedom for me. I tried on hat after hat to see which ones fit and which ones didn't. From the outside, other people might have seen me as flaky, unfocused, and even unsuccessful. But I knew otherwise. I was learning what made me happy, what stoked my inner flame, and what I could do to feel nourished and excited for the rest of my life.

When I decided that I wanted to help people create a life of freedom and joy through connection—connection to self, connection to other people, connection to the earth, and connection to something greater than themselves—the world opened up for me. People who were aligned with this vision serendipitously came into my life; I got a publishing contract with Hay House, which was my number one choice; and I was invited to events that resonated with my calling.

Knowing how to use your fire gives you the courage to move beyond your own fears and also helps you establish boundaries so that your flame doesn't get extinguished (or rage wildly out of control) by outside influences. As you start to explore your career and discover what your role is in the world, ask yourself these questions:

- Describe what you do for work? Are you self-employed or do you work for a company? Are you well paid? Is your job your passion? Would you do it if you didn't get paid? Do you feel like your work matters?

- Describe your workplace. What does it look like? What hours do you keep? With whom do you work? What kinds of things do you do on the job? How are people treated?

- Have you tapped into your internal fire or passion? Are you controlling it, or is it running wild? Is your spirit shining bright, or is it just a small ember waiting to be fanned to life? Is your life full of vitality and enthusiasm?

- Do you have hidden anger, rage, or frustration that could be holding you back from your best life?

- Are you living your dreams? Do you see yourself doing something else in the future? If so, what does it look like? How would you feel if you knew your life's purpose?

- What have you done in your life that you are proud of?

- Describe your leadership style? Do you see your work as a competition and a race to the top, or do you find win-win solutions for all involved? Do you value your ability to make a difference in the world?

- What do you love to do? Do you believe that you could make money doing this? Do you believe that this is a worthy vocation? Do you know others who are doing this in the world? What do you think about them?

- Do you own your power? Do you know how to use your personal power to help others? Describe how you balance this with your compassion and empathy?

- Describe where you find your joy in life? Describe how you would cultivate more. What does joy feel like to you? Do you believe that you could turn this activity into a vocation?

- Describe how you would act if you had the power to know what's right for you in every situation.

- Describe what would you do if you had the courage to be bold and live out all your dreams in all areas of your life.

- Who do you need to become in order to develop your vocation?

- Are you free to be yourself at work? Do you have the freedom to speak from your heart? Are you hiding parts of yourself?

When we aren't doing work that fuels our flame, we'll continually feel as if something's missing. It will seem that we're not living up to our potential; this fear will start to build up as resentment, anger, and rage, which can be explosive at times. Our job in life is to explore our vocation, and when we find it, put all our heart into it. So then when we're living our life's work, it doesn't feel like work at all. We'll feel as if what we do truly matters.

4. *Air:* Relationships

Both air and love are necessary to sustain life on the planet and in our Life Gardens. Positive relationships directly affect our level of happiness, and they yield tremendous joy and emotional and physical pleasure. Contrast that with toxic relationships (or the lack of important relationships altogether), which tend to produce stress, loneliness, and negativity.

Exploring the air in our Gardens means asking some questions about the quality of the relationships we currently have in our lives—with our parents, our romantic partners, our children, our co-workers, and our social network. It also means taking a look at the relationships we don't have and wish we did.

When I started to breathe the air in my own Life Garden, I realized I was a little oxygen deprived. I thought about why that might be and made some interesting discoveries. I came to understand that the reason I worked so hard, wasn't married, and clung to my relationships was because of a trauma I'd experienced in the past, which was still choking the air out of my Garden.

It sounds like an insignificant thing now that I've worked through it, but our perceptions of events can lead to very real and traumatic experiences. You see, I had a cyst removed from above my left eyebrow when I was a little girl, and this required that I stay in the hospital overnight without my parents by my side. Although I was less than two years old, I vividly remember this experience and can still clearly see my mom and dad walking down the hall, saying good night, and leaving me in this sterile hospital with strangers dressed in white—while I screamed at the top of my lungs for them not to leave me. In my mind at the time, my parents abandoned me. And even if it was just for a night, it had a profound effect on me.

I began to see that this one event had shaped my entire adult Garden. I still felt like that child, trying to fulfill the absence of parental nurturing. This is why I worked so hard for my boss's praise, this was why I clung to friendships so tightly, and this was why I held back from partners—I was afraid that they might abandon me, too.

This trauma was preventing me from forming the kinds of intimate connections that would make me happier and healthier.

In order to heal this wound, I enlisted the help of a holistic facilitator who enabled me to explore my relationship patterns with parents, boyfriends, friends, and colleagues. The facilitator helped me visualize and re-create the childhood scenario in my mind, but instead of being the abandoned little girl, I became the parent. I nurtured little Heather, took her home with me, and made sure that she was loved and taken care of. I was now her parent and she was me. This may sound unusual, but the process actually helped greatly. Along with my own self-care—eating right, sleeping eight hours per night, and taking warm baths—it allowed me to heal this trauma.

Here are some questions to ask yourself as you explore the air element in your garden:

- What are your beliefs about relationships? Do you place conditions on other people, such as parents, friends, or neighbors?

- What kinds of relationships do you have with others? Do you feel connected? Physically nurtured? Emotionally nurtured?

- Do your current relationships provide you with room to breathe, or are they stifling and controlling?

- Are you living from your head or your heart?

- Are you willing to do what it takes to have loving relationships?

- Are there past traumas that are preventing you from forming the kinds of relationships that will make you happy? Do you know what they are? Have you healed from these traumas?

- Are you gentle with yourself and the people in your life, or are you quick to pass judgment and criticism?

- What does your love relationship look like? How does it feel? What do you do together? How do you treat one another? Do you have expectations for this relationship?

- Do you have the relationships with your family and friends that you desire? What would you change? Describe whom you consider to be a part of your family. What kinds of activities do you do with them? How often do you see them? How do you treat one another?

- What does your social life look like? How much time do you spend time with your friends, and what do you tend to do together? How do you treat one another? Do you see all people as equals?

- How would your relationships change if you knew that they'd all be full of unconditional love and fulfillment?

- How willing are you to share your truth with others? Describe your communication style.

- How do you contribute to the community? How does your community change because of you?

- How is the relationship with yourself? How do you treat yourself?

- Do you believe that all living things are interconnected?

When we don't have clear air in our Life Gardens, we don't have the ability to give and receive love freely. We might have unrealistic expectations about relationships or have false beliefs. Once I healed from my traumatic childhood experience, for example, my father revealed to me that parents weren't allowed to stay at the hospital, and it was very difficult for them to leave me. Once I did my healing work internally, Dad brought this up without any prompting, and I was able to understand the truth of what happened.

When we're open to looking at our relationships, we can free ourselves from the past so that we can move forward in the future.

5. *Spirit:* Creative Expression

Creative expression is the spark of the divine, which is alive in you and at the heart of your Life Garden. It is the element of limitless possibilities. It is the soul of your Garden—the spirit that lives and expresses itself in each and every blossom. Your creative expression can include fun and recreation as well as your spiritual life. Spirituality is an integral element in every Life Garden; when you bring focused consciousness to your spiritual life, you gain power, clarity, and strength from inside that allows you to transcend space and time.

Although I'd always gone to church or participated in religious training, I did so because it was what everyone else did, it was a good thing to do, and it was something I wanted to believe in. I said the words and went through the motions, but I didn't *feel* anything. I really didn't understand how to have a personal relationship with God.

As I was searching for more meaning in my life, I started exploring different kinds of spiritual tools, teachers, and writings—and I found the angels. I'd always believed in angels, but it wasn't until I saw Doreen Virtue live that I really experienced the love and guidance of an angel. I don't remember exactly what she said that night, but I felt the love of angels all around me and could physically feel their presence. It was this belief in something that I couldn't see that opened my mind to something more. I started reading about angels, bought a deck of Doreen's angel cards, and even had "angel dinners" with some of my closest girlfriends to discuss our lives and ask the angels for guidance.

My new faith gave me comfort in knowing that I wasn't alone, and it also afforded me the courage to explore the boundaries of my beliefs and my creative potential. My creativity is expressed through communication, via both the written word and communicating one-on-one with other people. As I began speaking my truth, I learned more and more about who I was as a creative person and began to flourish. The more I tapped into the multidimensionality of life and sincerely connected with my spiritual self, the more confident and courageous I became. I started to do things differently, take risks, and realign my life.

◎

What is your form of creative expression in the world? Here are some questions to ask yourself as you explore the spirit element in your garden:

- Do you feel connected to something greater than yourself? Describe what you believe or know about your spirituality and what that feels like.

- What does your spiritual life look like? Are you involved in a church? Do you go on retreats? Do you meditate? Do you go out into nature?

- Do you feel uninspired and bored with life? Do you wonder if this is all there is?

- Do you allow yourself to imagine many possibilities? Can you visualize your life in the future? Can you picture being the person you dreamed of and having all the things that you desire?

- Do you know how to tap into your intuition? Do you trust your intuition or do you rely on logic and reason? Describe how you use your intuition.

- Do you have any unresolved grief, pride, fear, or jealousy that is holding you back from expressing yourself creatively?

- Do you have outlets for creative expression, fun, and recreation in your life—to the point that you lose a sense of time and space?

- Is there an activity that once brought you complete joy that you no longer include in your life? Why?

- What would you do if you knew anything was possible and that there were unlimited possibilities for creation and abundance? What would you come up with? What dreams would you make come true?

- Do you cultivate peace in your life? How important is it to you? Describe what gives you a sense of peace?

- Is your life guided by external controls and measures, or through an internal guidance system that's based on your feelings?

- Are you doing things to change the world? Do you feel the freedom to create and express yourself through your creations?

- Are you open to knowing who you really are?

- Do you feel that you have to do certain things in order to be loved by a higher power? Do you believe that you will be taken care of if you turn your life over to this higher power?

When we aren't authentically connected to something greater than ourselves—God, Allah, higher self, supreme power, energy, source, or consciousness—then we will never get access to our creative expression. Alignment with spirit gives us the genius to tap into our potential and possibilities in the world, along with the courage to explore those possibilities through our creative outlet. When we've tapped into our spirituality and the flow of creation, then we are full of joy, fulfillment, and freedom.

Planning Your Life Garden

Now that we've gone through the five main elements of your Life Garden as it is today, it's time to get clear about what you intend to create in your Garden of the future. It's important to write these plans down (or even draw them) so that you don't leave anything out when you start to develop your plan.

When you plan your Life Garden, you have to decide how you feel about what's there presently, and compare that to the Garden you'd really like to have. You might find that you love something that's there, but it's in the wrong location. Or you could discover that there are a lot of weeds around a rare and beautiful plant that hasn't been given any attention. Whatever you have right now, you need to do the work to clean up your current area, while at the same time start to sow the seeds and cultivate the Garden of your dreams in order to find what brings you joy.

By creating a plan for your individual Life Garden, you can create permanent positive changes in how you shape your life. So go back through the answers you jotted down in response to the questions in the last section, and examine the landscape of your life. What areas are not flourishing? What do you want to harvest in the future? Pay close attention to what feelings pop up as you review your answers. Which aspects of your life require more attention or nourishment? Overall, does your landscape look like the Garden that you envisioned for yourself? If not, what are the gaps? Now it's time to go through the same questions, but instead of answering them based on your current situation, spend time answering them based on what you want your life to look like. There are no boundaries, no limitations, and no rules. This is an exercise to get your mind thinking about the possibilities in life. You don't have to worry about how you're going to achieve it—you just have to identify what you want to plant.

Take your time to answer all the questions, and then write down how you want to feel in this new Life Garden. We'll use the answers for this exercise in the next chapter, but for now it's about exploring your mind, your desires, and your possibilities.

Like a natural garden, our lives are not static; they're constantly growing and evolving entities. We need to consistently weed out, shape up, and clear out the landscape so that it can grow and change and evolve over the course of our lives. We need to continually explore and challenge our beliefs, ask questions, and turn over the soil to discover new truths in order to maintain the Life Gardens of our dreams.

When we plant the seed of exploration, we offer ourselves the opportunity to take control of our own destiny, and choose what we want to sow and ultimately reap. The process of discovery can involve facing some difficult truths about our current environment, but the awareness allows us to clear away the weeds and cut back the over-grown plants that are shading out the young shoots so that new life is free to grow.

Sometimes all a garden needs is a little sculpting. Often with just the addition of a few colorful annuals, you can refresh the whole land-scape. Other times, however, as in my own Life Garden, you have to rip out big chunks because they've overgrown their beds so much that they're choking out all of the other plants. My process of explora-tion led me to quit my job, which left me with a lot of barren soil to plant. Today, though, where there was once a giant thornbush, there is now a whole new world of biodiversity taking root.

In this chapter, you planted the seed of exploration by examining the five aspects of your life and thinking about what you want your dream Life Garden to look like. When you explore what you like and don't like, it gives you the information to find out what matters to you; it gets you closer to finding your freedom.

In the next chapter, we'll plant the seed of focus and learn how to clear the way to cultivate what matters.

Digging Deeper: What Brings You Joy?

To dig deeper into the seed of exploration, you can:

1. Think like a child. Notice what you loved to do in your youth and see if it's something that still gives you enthusiasm. Did you paint? Water-ski? Garden? Play guitar in a band? Put on musicals? Cook? Decorate your bedroom? Play basketball? Draw comics? Help people in the community? Whatever it was, really explore that part of your life to see if that activity is something that still brings you joy.

2. Notice moments of joy. Pay attention to what makes you happy in your daily life: a good cup of tea, the sunrise on your way to work, a baby's laugh, giving a good sales presentation, running, reading, playing the piano, teaching a class, playing ball with your kids, writing poetry, or what have you. When you pay attention to the moments in life when you're in your own joy, you'll be able to identify what really matters to you.

3. Gather images and words. Keep a selection of words, images, cards, quotes, poems, and photographs that make you happy. You can print them off the Internet, use your own photographs, repurpose cards that people have given you, or rip pictures out of magazines. You'll want to collect images and words that inspire you and represent what you want to plant in your Life Garden and keep them in a folder, a beautiful envelope, a special box, or on a bulletin board. When you collect a variety of images and words, you can then start to see trends as far as what really matters.

CHAPTER TWO

FOCUS

"Every garden-maker should be an artist along his own lines. That is the only possible way to create a garden, irrespective of size or wealth."

— VITA SACKVILLE-WEST

In the first few months after I quit my job, I worked on planting the seed of focus in my Life Garden. At the time, this meant that I was focused on finding the right partner, getting married, and having kids. Dating became my number one priority. I was really enjoying meeting so many interesting people—and it was wonderful to have the time to actually be present for my dates, as well as to contemplate a romantic relationship and maybe even a family life. It was a great season in the garden, and I didn't want it to end. I was determined to grow my dream of a husband and children.

So when my friend Reshma asked me to go to India with her because her husband wasn't able to, my initial reaction was, *Wow, what a great opportunity!* It was so tempting because I'd recently rediscovered my passion for travel, and this wasn't just any old trip.

Reshma is a prominent marketing professor at Emory University's Goizueta Business School. About once a year she takes business leaders, students, or alumni (like me) on specialized trips to India to meet with leading business, political, and cultural leaders. For this particular visit, Reshma had plans to meet the country's president and prime minister, along with Bollywood producers and CEOs or top executives from the largest companies in India. This would be akin to meeting the President of the United States and the secretary of state; the CEOs of Wal-Mart, GE, Bank of America, Ford, and Delta Air Lines; and Hollywood producers. Yet my friend also assured me that there would be plenty of time to sightsee and experience the highlights of this amazing land. It sounded like the journey of a lifetime!

I was free and clear to enjoy a new adventure. But then I thought, *Well, I shouldn't spend the money when I don't have a stable income. And most important, I don't want to miss out on a month of dating activity.* So, although international travel was one of my greatest joys in life, I didn't think it was a prudent decision. I had a plan, and going to India was not part of that plan. I was starting to micromanage my garden.

It sounds silly now, but I really thought I could use my consulting and business skills to find a husband. My friends teased me because they said that I had a project plan to get married. I didn't actually have a spreadsheet on what to do, but I *was* pretty ambitious about going to social functions, getting in shape, looking my best, and doing a lot of inner work to attract the right kind of person. That's what all the self-help books on how to find a guy or fall in love said to do. And I did it.

Ultimately, my love of travel inspired me to say yes to going to India, and it turned out to be one of the most incredible experiences of my life. The combination of learning about a new culture, meeting with top business and political figures throughout the country, and engaging all my senses in something new and foreign was intoxicating. I barely slept the entire time because I wanted to do everything and experience all I could. My spirit had come alive!

Reshma and I ended up traveling all over the place for several weeks meeting with the heads of most of the preeminent businesses in the nation, such as Wipro, JetBlue Airways, the Birla Corporation, and Tata, to name a few. True to her word, Reshma also made time for us to enjoy the country's sights: the splendor of the Taj Majal, the beaches of Goa, and the majesty of Lake Palace in Rajasthan. We also had the excitement of searching for Bengal tigers in the Ranthambore National Park.

On one of our last days of the trip, I was sitting in the Rashtrapati Bhavan (the presidential palace of India), waiting for the president, Dr. A. P. J. Abdul Kalam, to join our small group for tea and a discussion about the economic and social growth in India. I was wearing a beautiful royal blue *salwar kameez,* a traditional Indian outfit I'd just purchased in one of the local sari shops, and I thought, *How did I get here?*

Just a few months earlier, I'd have been sitting in a windowless conference room decorated with one whiteboard, a phone, a conference table, and a few broken chairs, bouncing from meeting to meeting throughout the day. Now I was sitting in the largest official residence of any head of state in the world, that of the president of India in New Delhi. I was totally in the moment and realized that my amazement wasn't about the prestige, but more about the excitement of the trip and how the opportunity had unfolded. This incredible situation had presented itself to me unexpectedly, without my having to *do* anything. Was this really happening?

I was having such a wonderful time that I remember thinking how joyful I was in the moment. I didn't have a care in the world and was truly in a blissful state on each day of my Indian adventure. I'd connected with so many new friends, learned about the growing business and social economy in India, and thoroughly enjoyed exploring such a colorful and rich culture. Reshma and I whisked through the streets of Mumbai on rickshaws, rode elephants and camels in a royal procession, tried on colorful saris, and went on a safari. I was having more fun than I'd had in years.

By returning to something that had once been a great passion for me—travel—I was now nurturing all the best parts of myself. I was so energized that I started to see the world through new eyes, and my spirit started to return. I felt alive and full of hope and happiness. And that's when I met a man who changed my life. Here I'd thought that by going to India I'd be taking a break from the work I'd been doing to grow a family. But the Universe knew better than I did. As it turned out, following my joy brought me right where I'd wanted to be.

As you can see from this story, when we cultivate what makes us happy—our values, our dreams, and our joy—then whatever we're seeking has an opportunity to come into our lives. Whenever we're trying to make something happen or control the flow of the river of life, then the process is not fun . . . and we usually wind up exhausting ourselves swimming upstream, never getting anywhere despite our efforts.

Ted Ning's Story

Ted and I have been working together in various capacities for several years. What I admire most about him is that he really "walks the talk." As the leader of the LOHAS (Lifestyles of Health and Sustainability) Forum, Ted is passionate about bringing business, individuals, and organizations together for win-win solutions.

Ted's upbringing had a profound impact on how he views the world. He is the eldest of six children, three of which were adopted from Vietnam and Korea. Ted's mother and father developed a successful nonprofit organization that provided medical aid and microcredit loans in Southeast Asia and Central America. Through his parents' humanitarian work, he was exposed to the world of poverty and the underserved at a young age. He learned about philanthropy and microfinance, as well as how much education and improved health can help the poor.

As a teen, Ted traveled to China, Mongolia, Russia, and Europe, which opened his eyes to different cultures and viewpoints. This started him on his journey of interconnecting humanity and the planet, and he's been involved in community outreach and nonprofit work ever since.

Ted's life path has taken him many places, and he's the first to admit that the path has had some twists, turns, and bumps—just like his skiing. Yes, he's an outdoor enthusiast and was even a ski coach during the 1998 Nagano Winter Olympics. He also has a passion for education, which led him to acquire a master's degree in adult education and to teach English in Japan and Vietnam.

Ted sees a need for businesspeople (and adults in general) to bring more passion, fun, and excitement into their work. He wants to share his knowledge of health, sustainability, and adult education with businesses to help them create more productive meetings, more collaborative business relationships, and more meaningful connections. He's watched the $290 billion LOHAS marketplace explode over the past few years, yet he's also seen businesses struggle with effective communication strategies that provide solutions for all stakeholders involved: consumers, business owners, strategic partners, vendors, employees, and stockholders; along with the earth, the silent stakeholder. Ted feels that by integrating the LOHAS values into our corporate culture and personal lives, we can all provide solutions that are not only good for business, but also healthy for consumers and sustainable for the planet.

Both personally and professionally, Ted's journeys have exposed him to the foremost leaders in the world on spirituality, health, wellness, sustainability, and lifestyle. He sees that big business has the responsibility and the opportunity to do what's right and take a leadership position by being true to companies' values. It's not enough for business to focus solely on growth, the bottom line, and unlimited resources. By concentrating on "values based" cultures, companies can improve their profitability, create better products, and foster healthier work environments. This way, all stakeholders win.

Today, Ted continues to lead the mission of LOHAS by writing articles, speaking at conferences worldwide, and connecting businesspeople and individuals who can work together toward a common goal. Even though this extraordinary man has always cared about the well-being of others on a personal level, it's taken him time to gather the courage to bring that sensitive quality to his work as well—but his patience and diligence have paid off. Ted trusts his intuition and spiritual connection, and he makes sure that he's always living his values as he conducts his business. He knows that he has a role to play and understands his purpose of connecting people, ideas, and concepts for a better tomorrow. He heavily relies on his gut instinct, has compassion for people regardless of their external circumstances, and is able to be authentic in his business.

Ted really does walk the talk. He currently resides outside of Boulder, Colorado, with his wife and dog. There, he rides his bike to work; gets his meals from community-supported organic farms; recycles his trash and composts his waste; and lives in a green-built home, which is powered by solar energy. Professionally, he gets carbon offsets for his travel, stays in "green" hotels, carries his own coffee mug and water bottle, and ensures that the events he produces are adding to the world—mentally, physically, and spiritually.

We don't turn off who we are at the doorstep of our offices. If we recycle, we need to integrate that into our work; if we want to eat healthfully, then we need to provide nutritious alternatives at meetings; and if we believe in our integrity, then we need to make sure that our professional agreements are also done in alignment with our personal beliefs. This is the new way of business, and Ted's example of leadership is a great example for us all.

What Matters to You?

Planting the seed of focus in your life involves becoming clear about what your values are. What matters to you? What do you hold in high regard? What do you respect and require in your life? What can't you live without (or with)?

Your core values are the things you rate most crucial in your life. They're what influence the choices you make, the way you behave, the kinds of people you choose to interact with, and the way you spend your time. So would you say that beauty, freedom, love, abundance, or productivity are most important to you? Or do you prefer to have fun or pay attention to detail? However you respond, note that your Life Garden should always reflect the essence of your core values, so cultivating relationships with whatever you hold dear is at the bedrock of a healthy Garden. Exploring your values is also a good way to tap into the essence of who you are right *now*.

On the next page, there are a number of core values. Please look at each word or phrase in the list and consider it carefully. If you feel that it describes what you value most in life, write it down in your journal or notebook. Be sure to only choose the words that you *value;* that is, those which are really important in all aspects of your life. Remember that we all embody many of these words, so be a bit discriminating and don't write down every single one. You may also add any of your own if you don't see them listed.

Now, go through all the words you wrote down and select ten that are critical to have in your life. Write those ten words on a new page in your journal.

Next, you're really going to tap into your inner self and find out what matters most to you. From the previous list, select the three to five words that are absolutely essential to have in your life—these represent the essence of who you are. That is, if you had to pick three or four words to describe what you value most in life, what would they be? Write those words on a new page in your journal.

You can use your words to start the creation of your Life Garden. There are no good or bad, right or wrong, or should-have words. These are merely tools to help you discover what you personally value—and since your Garden is uniquely yours, it doesn't have to look like anyone else's or what your mother, husband, or boss thinks it should look like.

Values List

Abundance	Delightfulness	Honesty	Optimism	Serenity
Acceptance	Dependability	Honor	Organization	Service
Achievement	Devotion	Humanity	Passion	Sexuality
Activity	Dignity	Humor	Patience	Sincerity
Adventure	Discernment	Imagination	Peacefulness	Solitude
Affection	Discipline	Impact	Perfection	Space
Amusement	Drama	Importance	Order	Spirituality
Artistic ability	Dreaming	Improvement	Organic	Sports
Aspiration	Duty	Independence	Playfulness	Stability
Attentiveness	Education	Individuality	Pleasure	Status
Attractiveness	Efficiency	Influence	Politeness	Stimulation
Authority	Elegance	Information	Popularity	Strength
Autonomy	Encouragement	Ingenuity	Possessions	Structure
Awareness	Energization	Initiative	Possibilities	Success
Balance	Energy	Innovation	Power	Support
Beauty	Enjoyment	Inquisitiveness	Predictability	Sustainability
Belonging	Enlightenment	Inspiration	Preparation	Talent
Bliss	Enterprise	Intelligence	Presence	Taste
Bravery	Entertainment	Integration	Professionalism	Teaching
Building	Excellence	Integrity	Providing	Tenacity
Capability	Exhilaration	Interconnectivity	Punctuality	Tenderness
Change	Facilitation	Inventiveness	Quality	Thoughtfulness
Clarity	Fame	Joy	Questioning	Tolerance
Coaching	Family	Justice	Radiance	Tradition
Collaboration	Financial security	Knowledge	Realization	Training
Comfort	Forthrightness	Laughter	Reason	Tranquility
Commitment	Freedom	Leadership	Recognition	Transformation
Community	Friendship	Learning	Refinement	Travel
Compassion	Fulfillment	Logic	Relating to God	Triumph
Competence	Fun	Love	Relaxation	Trustworthiness
Competition	Generosity	Loyalty	Reliability	Truthfulness
Completeness	Giving	Magnificence	Religiousness	Understanding
Connection	Glamour	Mastery	Respectfulness	Uniqueness
Contentment	Government	Meditation	Responsibility	Unity
Contribution	Grace	Ministry	Risk	Uplifting
Control	Gratitude	Moving forward	Romance	Variety
Cooperation	Growth	Mystery	Routine	Vitality
Courage	Happiness	Nature	Satisfaction	Vulnerability
Creativity	Hard work	Nourishment	Searching	Wealth
Danger	Harmony	Nurturing	Security	Winning
Decisiveness	Health	Observation	Sensitivity	Wisdom
Dedication	Helpfulness	Open-mindedness	Sensuality	Wonder

When I did this exercise, I discovered that my top four values are: *connection, freedom, creativity,* and *joy.* These four words describe my essence. For example, I know that connection—with self, a higher power, and other people—is so essential to me that it's how I'm guided in my life. I also know that freedom is one of my highest values because I want to live life on my terms; I'm much happier when I don't have the confines of a job, structure, or rules telling me what to do. Creativity is another important value for me because I'm at my best when I'm creating, organizing, and improving all of the possibilities in life. I am an idea person and need to express these ideas through any type of creation. Creating is easy and fun for me. And finally, I want to be able to let my light shine for the whole world to see. I want to experience joy in all that I do—beautiful things, positive people, and uplifting situations in the world. When I share my four words, people automatically confirm that I've picked out the right ones for my personality. These words create my personal and professional culture, and everything I do in life focuses on them.

Once you've identified your own core values, it becomes much easier to begin to cultivate those values in your Life Garden. If you value beauty, then perhaps you'll plant lots of roses. If you value service, then you may start a community garden that services a local food bank. Or, like me, you may discover that you want to grow a family—and wind up riding a camel in India. We all have our own ways of expressing values. We can use our unique gifts and roles in the world to create our own Gardens. When we recognize that each person truly is an individual expression, then we have the freedom to construct our own lives based on what brings us joy.

As you start to cultivate your Garden based on your values, you may focus on a specific skill, growth area, or aspect of yourself and find that your life—and everything in it—begins to change and evolve. This could include the people you associate with, the things you care about, the music or television programs you like, the clothes you wear, how you spend your time and resources, or even how much money you make. All this change has residual effects. Your friends may not like what's happening and stop inviting you to parties; your spouse may not like your new body; you might not be able to afford the vacations that your family is planning this summer—or you *can* now afford things that your neighbors can't.

If you're true to your values and know that what you're doing is right for your life, you'll be able to handle these changes. As you get to know yourself better, you'll become more firmly rooted in who you really are and what you want from life. And you'll be able to manage these changes as well. You don't have to stay at the same job, keep the same friends, or continue to do the same activities throughout your life; it's natural for these things to change as you do. It's a part of the transformational process as you become more focused.

Your Mission and Your Vision

Once you've identified your core values, the next step is to use this information to help identify your mission. I found it helpful to actually write a statement for myself that was short, sweet, and easy to remember, because I like to repeat it to myself often. I know that I'm passionate about helping and connecting people, so using my four values, I created the following mission statement:

> To help people live a life of *freedom* and *joy* through *connection* and *creativity.*

Now write your own mission statement—a declaration of what you stand for and what you want to be for the world—that truly reflects your top four core values. Keep it with you and look at it often. Even memorize it if you can, so you can repeat it to yourself when the soil gets rocky and you need to be reminded of what all your work is about.

Next, imagine your life with no boundaries. As Albert Einstein once said, "Imagination is everything." You are totally free to be, have, or do anything you want. There are no rules, there are no controls, and there are no limits. Everything you desire in life is possible. So if all of this is true, and anything *is* possible, what would your Life Garden look like?

Developing your vision is an opportunity to live in your optimal desired state. It's the expression of your deepest desires regardless of your current circumstances. Your vision is important because it allows you to give yourself permission to imagine and experience absolute freedom from all limitations.

When I first started thinking about my own vision, I realized that I was so disconnected from what I really wanted in life, I didn't even know where to start. So I just started writing stream-of-consciousness style to see where my thoughts would take me. I thought, *What would I want my life to look like if I knew I couldn't fail?* Here's a condensed version of what I wrote:

I see myself married to a wonderful man. He is intelligent, loyal, hardworking, handsome, and funny. We work together in some way that allows us to have a more flexible schedule. I could continue consulting for Fortune 500 companies, or we could start an entirely new business together; however, I do see us in some kind of entrepreneurial venture. (I would also like to continue buying investment real-estate properties.) We are endeavoring to save money for the future and are focused on building our financial security. We believe in hard work and long hours, but we also enjoy taking time off to spend with family and friends, as well as to travel and just enjoy life.

I see us having at least two healthy children and a dog. I see myself staying home with our kids while I continue to work in the business. Being a mom is extremely important to me, and I want to be there for my children and all of their activities. We are fit and enjoy sports and outdoor activities as part of our lifestyle. I like to cook and provide nutritious meals for my family.

I see us living in a beautiful home in Atlanta, where we enjoy playing tennis and golf. We also love to spend time outdoors, biking, hiking, and camping as a family and with our friends. Our house is where all the kids want to hang out because we have a great basement, lots of toys and games, and a pool. I also see us also having a home in Hilton Head Island, South Carolina, so that we can be near my parents and get away to the beach for the weekend with the kids. I want my children to know their grandparents, and it's important that we have the flexibility to spend time together.

We go to church on Sunday, attend Sunday school with the kids, and volunteer in the community. Giving back and commu-nity service are important values in our family.

As a single woman with a successful career, that was the only thing I really desired in my life. If you let yourself get completely car-ried away, what would you envision for yourself? Grab your journal and a pen and sit in a quiet area where you won't be disturbed. Then say good-bye to all of your limitations and preconceptions, and just start writing a vision of your future life. Write until you've completely run out of future blessings to count. Don't worry about any obstacles or blocks that pop into your head—write through them.

As you describe your vision, be aware of the limitless abundance and possibilities in the world. *Everything* is possible, and you have all of the resources available to create your dream life. As you write, make sure to keep all of your statements present-focused and affirmative, basing them on how you want to feel. For example: *I feel beautiful and vibrant. I am happy when I think about others first. I am appreciative for all of the good in my life.*

You can also create a vision board or online scrapbook with visuals of what you want to create or feel. Visuals are very powerful to help add imagery to what you want to create in your Life Garden; in this way, you can bring it to actual life when the time comes.

Now ask your inner self, *Is this my purpose? Does what I wrote really matter to me?* Don't think about an answer, but wait to see what kind of response you get. Remember not to think about it. You may get flashes of images, a scent, or a feeling that you're on the right track; or you might get an image or words about something entirely different. Play around with this exercise. The more you can visualize yourself living your purpose, the more aligned you'll be with your inner self and the more joy and excitement you'll feel for where you're going.

Once you've created a mission, a vision, and a purpose for your life, the next step in cultivation is to keep this vision and purpose clearly before your eyes and in your heart as you begin to bring your vision to life in the garden. When I was focusing on the creation of my own Life Garden, I'd spend 15 minutes every morning visualizing my new life, with me at the center of a brand-new Life Garden. I found this exercise very helpful at these early stages of my transformation, so I wanted to share it with you.

Exercise: Daily Focus

1. Find or create a quiet place without any disruptions for at least 15 minutes. Make sure that your phone is off.

2. Get into a relaxed position and close your eyes.

3. Bring consciousness to your breathing, concentrating on your inhales and exhales.

4. Play some ambient or spa music with headphones. (There are some tracks that are specifically designed to work in harmony with your brain, such as those that are available through **www.centerpointe.com,** but you can also find ambient music on iTunes or Pandora. Note that you'll want to look for tracks that are about 60 beats per minute.)

5. Read your vision statement and look at any visuals that elicit how you want to *feel.* Read it again and imagine what your vision would *taste* like. Read it again and imagine what your vision would *smell* like. Read it again and imagine what your vision would *look* like. Read it again and imagine what your vision would *sound* like. Read it again and imagine yourself in that situation, going through your daily activities, and hold a clear image of *all your senses.*

6. Feel this place with your heart and remember *why* you want this. Once it's clear, let it go. (If what you want and what you believe don't match, the seeds that you've planted and your desires for your Garden won't grow. When you feel *and* know that something will happen, then you'll see results.)

7. Say thank you and release your vision to your higher power.

The Power of Positive Thinking

The vision of what you want to cultivate in your Life Garden may seem far away from where you're currently standing. What you've envisioned might appear impossible and out of reach thanks to financial obstacles, talent limitations, geographical barriers, the life stage you're in, a controlling person, or a lack of education. Yet whenever you imagine an obstacle, you must immediately think more positive thoughts, as they're vital for making your Garden a reality.

Human beings think about 60,000 thoughts each day. When we write out our vision statements, we're telling our subconscious mind that these thoughts are more important than all of our other thoughts combined. Our mind then starts to focus on these thoughts and tries to find evidence to support them. It's like a miniature search engine in the brain, finding all the connections to make our visions a reality.

Have you ever noticed that when someone points out a new car you've never seen or heard of before, you suddenly see that car everywhere? Well, that car has been there all along, but your subconscious has simply brought it to your attention. When you understand how powerful your subconscious mind can be, you can use that power quite effectively in the creation of your Life Garden.

As you plan the type of Garden that you want to experience, you can also train your thoughts away from your current landscape. Keep in mind that no matter what you plant in your Garden, the idea starts in the fertile ground of your imagination. So if you're complaining about all that you're lacking, then you will never attract what you really want. You need to develop the good in your life first through your thoughts and words, and then you'll be in a place to receive that good.

So what are you cultivating?

- Scarcity or abundance?

- Sickness or health?

- Control or freedom?

- Fear or love?

- Boredom or creative expression?

Cultivating abundance, health, freedom, love, and creative expression takes effort. Just like in a real garden, ugly weeds grow freely, but to grow a beautiful rose or prizewinning squash, we need to give it the good stuff: soil, water, fertilizer, and care. Weeds and pests must be removed or they'll threaten the well-being of the garden's health.

Listen to the words you use: Do you hear yourself complaining? Talking in a negative tone? Bemoaning your lack of money? Going on about how sick you are? How poorly people treat you? How much you hate your job? How you don't have enough time? How bad the economy is? How fat you are? How no one loves you? How life will never change? And how much time do you spend appreciating, praising, and being grateful for what you already have?

When you think and speak from a negative place, then you'll continue to attract that negativity—but when you hold positive thoughts in your mind, your body and actions will catch up with these thoughts, and it will be easy to make the changes that you want to make. As you remove the weeds of self-doubt, pessimism, and fear, you'll train your mind to focus on what you really want and who you really are. Before you know it, you'll start to feel better and unearth the real you, the one who can flourish and grow in the Garden of your creation. By creating what you want and how you want to feel in your mind first, then you're able to move forward toward freedom and release the resistance to any change or conformity. You're free to be your true self in your Garden.

When we focus on our Life Gardens, we're creating the opportunity for the ideal relationship, job, or financial situation to come to us. We want to cultivate well-being for all areas of our life. By developing these positive aspects, it's like giving our Gardens the fertilizer they need, and we release resistance to growth and change.

However, if we have deep-rooted beliefs about scarcity or fear, they're often hidden under the ground and we're not even conscious of them. We may have automatic responses (such as "I should," or "I have to") or blaming tendencies when we're faced with these beliefs. Yet we can reprogram our minds by intentionally saying yes to life and holding thoughts of well-being. Our thoughts cultivate what will be created in our lives. So when we say, "I appreciate my job," our minds work hard to create that reality.

The seed of focus is about creating the environment and improving your life through labor, care, and study. It takes strength and hard work to turn over and break up old patterns, but when you harvest the fruit of your labors, it will be worth it. You'll be using the power of your mind to focus on what you desire, and you'll consequently release resistance to allow your desired Life Garden to naturally grow. As it keeps growing and flourishing, you'll feel better and better—and then it's easy to leave behind those old ways that aren't working.

Cultivate Your Beliefs

Like the sun viewed through rose-colored glasses, our beliefs can be colored by our current environment. The prism of our circumstances can prevent us from objectively seeing the truth. We may feel that we should be spared the experience of a broken heart, getting fired, becoming ill, or losing our financial security, but that's not going to happen. And, in fact, the contrast between the "good" and "bad" parts of human existence serve us very well.

Whenever we try something out—be it a job, a relationship, an activity, or a vegetable from the garden—we know whether we like it or not. And when we know what we don't like, then it helps us figure out what we *do* like. Contrast helps us narrow down our choices in life, but we need to start experiencing that contrast in order to know what we genuinely do want to include in our Life Gardens.

Developing our beliefs means that we need to dig deeper than we have been in order to understand what we believe and why. It's through personal experience and trial and error that we can know what we truly value—then we can carefully select the thoughts and actions that are aligned accordingly. As we lean in the direction of the values that we want to embody, and then gradually practice these values, they will become a natural part of our lives and personality.

This process can also bring us closer to spirituality. As Pierre Teilhard de Chardin, the famous French philosopher and Jesuit priest, famously noted: "We are not human beings having a spiritual experience; we are spiritual beings having a human experience."

Human beings have a physical self of *doing* and a spiritual self of *being*. We're really good at the physical part, but not so good at the spiritual part. When we start to develop our Life Gardens, we're connecting to our essence and getting to know who we really are, what we like, what inspires us, what gives us enthusiasm, what makes us feel connected to the world, what our gift to share with the world is, what makes us feel free, and what brings us joy. Just like the plants in our gardens, our lives become about letting things happen and grow naturally. When we look at life from this spiritual perspective, it certainly changes the nature of who we really are—we shift from just *doing* to *being* as well.

Jamie's Story

I first met Jamie at a seminar I was hosting. She's an artist, and her business had been severely affected by the economy over the past few years. As the single mother of two girls, she'd been living on a modest income and hadn't updated her wardrobe in a very long time, except for an occasional accessory here and there when it was absolutely necessary. Financial security was at the top of her list of concerns and affected every aspect of her life, creating a continual downward spiral.

In order to get out of this constricting pattern, I recommended that Jamie change things up a bit and start living a more creative life, instead of just dreaming about it. One day she went through her closet and combined different pieces of clothing to create an outfit that she named "Silver Fox," which was inspired by a J. Crew catalog. Instead of going out and buying something new, Jamie found several pieces of clothing that she never would have put together—a sparkly top layered over a couple of T-shirts, multiple strands of jewelry, evening shoes in the day, and a scarf tied around her head.

One part of this woman loved the untethered creativity that she was expressing with this outfit, but the other part felt silly and unprofessional. She timidly went out into the world to see what the reaction would be. Jamie was cultivating her "inner artist" and decided that if she truly wanted to be successful at her chosen vocation, then she needed to pull off wearing "creative" outfits that inspired her.

As Jamie went about her day, something happened. Instead of wearing a basic outfit that no one noticed, everyone seemed to notice this ensemble. Her clients complimented on how stylish she looked, random people commented on what great energy she had, and her kids thought she was the coolest mom ever. She even met someone who commissioned an art piece from her that day.

Jamie realized that she could pull off more creative outfits instead of dressing in business clothes, and her energy shifted in kind. Her inner sense of security had changed, and that directly changed her outer experience. Jamie learned to be more true to her real self.

What are *you* yearning to express? Maybe you want a new hairdo, or to start wearing red cowboy boots or a Hawaiian shirt to work. Whatever it is, do it, and notice what happens. How do people react to you, and how do you feel?

Dare to Dream

When you align your thoughts, emotions, and actions with your higher self, then you can also align with your purpose and ultimately tap into the meaning of life. When you're standing in your own power and living out your purpose, you're living an authentic life, and people may wonder how you do it.

As I've tried to point out in this chapter, anything you create in your outer world begins in your mind first. When you learn to control your thoughts and start to imagine possibilities, dormant forces will awaken and grow inside of you to help turn those thoughts into reality. So, dare to dream! It's time to stop spending so much time making a living, and start spending time on creating your Life Garden.

Once you figure out your mission in life, then your Garden comes alive and has meaning and purpose, especially if that mission is aligned with something greater than yourself. You become so guided toward your mission that your mind, body, and soul work together to help you achieve whatever you're working on—be it a cause, purpose, or project.

I'm not saying that you need to do anything radical, but when you plant the seed of focus in your Life Garden, you *can* start taking risks every day. You've got to do something different—shake it up, do something uncomfortable, or clear out the clutter—whatever you do will help you see new possibilities. When you move out of your comfort zone, you get in touch with your true potential. It's time to quit being so practical and begin to do things you've always wanted to do that are aligned with what you value.

I've met men and women who have challenged management to start new and innovative programs at work, quit their corporate jobs in exchange for nonprofit work, left Wall Street for Main Street, had a baby and then started a business, left a secure job in technology to sail the Caribbean, and created beautiful artwork in retirement. All of these people are now flourishing in all areas of their Life Gardens. When *you* take the time to discover your gifts and have the courage to take action, then you will begin to create your own spectacular Garden, which you can share with the world.

Now that you've planted the seed of focus and have figured out what you want to grow in your Life Garden, the next step is to get yourself rooted. Once you have that strong foundation in place, then your dream Garden can start to grow in earnest.

Digging Deeper: The Power of Intention

To dig deeper and understand the power of intention as you develop your Life Garden, you can:

1. Notice your intention. Pay attention to what you say and do. Note that the intention behind something is just as important as the action itself. As you start to bring awareness to your intention behind your own actions—why you want something or why you're doing things a particular way—then you can see if that intention is aligned with what you want in your Garden.

2. Read *The Power of Intention* by Dr. Wayne W. Dyer. Your intention is your connection to the Universe, the power of the energy that exists in and around you. Dr. Dyer shows you how to connect the force of intention to help you live a better life, explaining that using the power of intention is a way to help you "feel good." If you're interested in reading more about this power and how to cultivate it in your Life Garden, then I highly recommend reading this book.

3. Share your intention. Go to **www.intent.com** to connect with other people who are setting intentions in their lives. Changing the way you think is really difficult, but when you have a community of like-minded people rooting you on, it makes the change that much easier.

CHAPTER THREE

ROOTING

"If we surrendered to earth's intelligence
we could rise up rooted, like trees."

— RAINER MARIA RILKE

You might think that in order to create a flourishing Life Garden, you need to work long hours and force things to happen. That's how many of us have been successful in our lives—we *make* things happen. We plan the kids' school activities, we take on additional projects at work, or we lead successful fund-raising campaigns for our favorite charities. We know how to get things done, and we're good at it. And if we're not good at it, there are thousands of books, articles, and teachers that instruct us how to do so, step-by-step.

We live in a society focused on doing, acting, and working hard; and we're often externally rewarded for this effort through raises, accolades, and praise. However, *Seeds of Freedom* is not about doing anything; it's about digging deep within ourselves to find a place of stillness so that we can listen to what's in our heart, know our own truth, and soak up the nourishment that fills us.

Most often we see life as a linear process: we're born, we go to school, we get married and have kids, we work, we have fun, and then we die. Yet if we're on a quest to find freedom in our lives, then we're searching for something more—a purpose, a calling, a reason for being. This causes us to reach deep into the unknown, so we're then able to expand our lives from linear to multidimensional, expanding past our five senses and up toward a higher consciousness.

We all contain seeds inside of us that are just waiting for the right time to open up and grow. The conditions must be just so for germination, and every one of us has different circumstances that will allow this to happen. These seeds may even lie dormant for a while as they wait for the right conditions to develop. The process takes time, patience, and simply sitting still—but if we're sincerely trying to find our truth and life purpose, we don't mind. We know that our seeds must crack open and grow roots before we'll be able to access our own unique calling and transform.

It's through this rooting in our increased awareness that we can see the infinite possibilities that exist in the world. We can then tap into the knowledge that anything is possible.

Henna Inam's Story

Henna had just left her executive position at a corporation and started a business that focused on helping women leaders transform themselves, their organizations, and their communities. That's when a former colleague of mine introduced us. Henna and I connected immediately since we shared the same vision for life and had similar professional backgrounds. Right away, I saw that she was redefining what it means to be a powerful and successful woman. She'd found the courage to reach deep within, become connected, and forge a path to living a free and more authentic life.

Henna has always had two sides to her: one, the very practical achiever and corporate-ladder climber; and the other, the spiritual seeker fascinated with "consciousness." Although she was raised as a Muslim in her home country of Pakistan, she was educated in a convent school early in life, as it was the best education around. Her parents—her father an oil executive and her mother a medical doctor—always made school a priority for their two girls. When Henna was 11, her family left their native land and spent various years in Tanzania, the Philippines, and Thailand before making their way to Texas when she was 19. She was exposed to many different cultures and faiths and learned the value of helping others early on, with her mother (who worked with Mother Teresa's orphanages) leading by example.

Henna also learned the value and necessity of having time to herself. A precocious and curious child, she was quite a voracious reader. She happily delved into imaginary worlds where she could contemplate lives and dimensions existing beyond her own. As a young woman, she completed her undergraduate degree at The University of Texas at Austin and went on to earn an MBA at The Wharton School of the University of Pennsylvania. Following graduation, she began a highly successful career with Procter & Gamble, which took her to Hong Kong (she then returned to the States and lived in Cincinnati, Ohio).

After seven years with Procter & Gamble, Henna left to start her career with Novartis, one of the largest global pharmaceutical companies. She'd spend the next 13 years there in positions of increasing responsibility in marketing, sales, and general management, eventually becoming chief marketing and innovation officer at CIBA Vision and the head of e-innovation for Novartis. It wasn't until later in her career that she realized she wanted to create a new path of both success and legacy.

As she explained, some of her most satisfying and illuminating decisions have been those made with her gut and intuition, rather than the traditional notions of logic and rationality. Therefore, when presented with the opportunity to take charge of sales for a billion-dollar business or accept the challenge of turning around a smaller one, she chose the latter. After visiting the company's operations in Mexico, Henna felt compelled to take on the assignment. Although the larger business represented more power and prestige in many respects, her gut told her that she needed to do this; she felt exhilarated by the opportunity.

Henna's two years in Mexico were some of the most fun and successful of her career, and she flourished. She and her team turned the business around, a key competitor ended up leaving the market, and they also won a highly coveted corporate award for their performance that's given to only 10 out of 90,000 associates worldwide. Henna was doing great professionally, but the achievement was not as fulfilling as she had hoped.

One night while flipping through the channels on TV, she came upon a documentary about child trafficking between Nepal and India. The story featured a woman who'd been sold into prostitution and managed to escape both her captors and the shame of her past. This woman had turned her own personal devastation into a mission to help others—she'd opened a halfway house on the border between Nepal and India to provide a safe haven for others who wanted to escape prostitution and begin a new life.

Henna had an epiphany: she realized that this former prostitute had found something that had thus far eluded her. She broke down in tears because she realized that for most of her life, she'd been seeking external achievements. This woman on TV was so much more powerful; she'd not only found a purpose, but a means to help others learn to help themselves. Although Henna was highly successful in almost every traditional sense and had all the associated material perks, her inner voice told her that her reason for being had not yet been fulfilled. It was at that moment that she embarked on a journey to find her own passion and purpose by listening to her inner voice.

This wasn't something that happened immediately. It took her four years from that night to set forth on her new path of freedom; in the meantime, she continued to explore the path she was currently on.

After 20 years in corporate positions, Henna left her role at Novartis and started her own company that focuses on helping female leaders transform themselves, their organizations, and their communities by tapping into their own innate wisdom and power. While each day brings a new challenge and opportunity, Henna has never been as fulfilled as she is today, as she is truly pursuing her passion.

The Growth That Happens Out of Sight

When we first decide to create our Life Gardens, we don't yet have enough sustenance to grow even a tiny little acorn. Our root system needs time to establish itself into the soil of our core beliefs, which will ultimately supply the nutrients necessary to sustain a great big oak tree.

Keep in mind that growth begins beneath the soil in places we can't see; a lot is happening there that is vital to the future strength and vitality of what we've planted. To that end, when a seed begins to grow, the first thing to burst from this bundle of energy is not a shoot that grows up, but a root that reaches down into the earth.

The root system is the lifeline for most plant life. It provides the nourishment for growth, stores reserve nutrients to carry a plant through times of scarcity, and serves as the foundation to prevent it from falling over or losing soil at its base. The same is true for us in our Life Gardens. Transformation begins by digging down for the energy we need to spring upward. Deep roots provide a firm foundation for the personal and spiritual growth to come. If an oak shoots up without first establishing its roots, its own weight will inevitably bring it down. Sturdy roots allow the tree to grow tall and survive the blustery winds in order to reach for the heavens. In the same way, our own strong roots can help us weather even the most terrible storms and setbacks.

It takes a long time for a seed to become a towering tree—again, it takes patience. It may look as if what we've planted in our Gardens isn't growing, but it is, inch by inch and day by day. We just have to trust the process, knowing that as our roots develop within us, we'll be able to grow in countless ways. This growth may not be visible to others, but *we* will feel the shifts internally by the way we feel and how we view the world. We'll begin to feel more centered, anchored, peaceful, and in tune with our surroundings. Our intuition will become more acute, our love and compassion for all living things will increase, and we'll know that we're on the right path despite any external barriers.

We all have roots in our personal stories, our family history, and our culture. And we all have secrets and mysteries lying beneath our external appearance. It's when we dig in and develop our own internal root system that we become more still, more aware, more peaceful, and more silent. In our Life Gardens, our roots become grounded in the bigger, unseen parts of ourselves that nourish the soul. Therefore, the higher we want to go and the bigger our dreams are, the deeper our roots need to be.

We encounter all of the seasons in our Gardens. After the warmth and joy of summer, we see autumn, with its flaming beauty, burn out. And in the depth of winter, it may look as if all we're left with is a withered landscape, a naked tree, or leaf-covered flower beds . . . but hidden from our view is the life that will grow and bloom in the spring. The seasons teach us that nature holds a mystery. We can see that our Gardens are not static; instead, they're continually changing and evolving. There's also much more happening beneath the surface than we can observe with our five senses. When we allow these deeper mysteries to exist in our Gardens, then we can open up all sorts of possibilities for our future.

It's important to trust that our Life Gardens will flourish, and to remain open to the magic that wants to assist us in our creation. Yet many of us are trying to control every single aspect of our Gardens and don't allow that magic, that natural growth, to occur organically. If we can anchor ourselves in stillness, our roots will bring nourishment up to our hearts and they will open, bringing us a glimpse of our interconnection with the world around us. It's when we have an open heart that we trust and allow nature's mystery to unfold.

The seed of rooting gives us freedom: Roots give us strength so that we can fear less and trust more. Roots give us flexibility so that we can control less and allow more. Roots give us access to the mystery of life so that we need proof less and allow possibilities and magic more. Roots give us the confidence that our gardens will grow, and a sense of knowing that there are things beneath the surface that we do not have to understand—but that give us life.

Opening Our Hearts and Clearing Our Minds

Although I love to connect deeply with people, doing so romantically didn't always come easily to me. Maybe I was scared of being intimate or getting hurt, but I always stayed busy and had things to do, which then kept me from entering into loving and intimate relationships. I was comfortable with my left-brain, logical view of the world and failed to realize that I wasn't rooted in the certainty of my heart.

As I mentioned earlier in the book, when I started cultivating my Life Garden, my initial intention was to grow a family. I wanted to be in love, get married, have kids, and live happily ever after. So I tried out different things to meet a man—dating, dancing, and flirting. It was a lot of fun, and I was learning a lot about myself. And then when I went to India, I met someone who was completely the opposite of what I'd had in mind for my Life Garden at that time.

My left brain said, *No, this isn't the guy.* But my right brain said, *Why not? What's holding you back? Just have some fun and see if you like him. Here's your chance to open your heart; connect to someone else; and, most important, grow. What are you waiting for?*

So I went for it and ended up falling in love. Our connection was instant and exciting. This relationship was unlike any I'd had before, and it was exhilarating. Although we were different in lots of ways, we were compatible in so many others. We spent all our time together—and it was easy, fun, loving, and sweet. Since we both wanted to have a family, it wasn't long before we were planning our future. I thought for sure that the seed I'd planted was growing.

But what was once wonderfully sensual, exciting, and beautiful became heart wrenching, agonizing, and ultimately toxic. You see, what I thought was a once-in-a-lifetime romance ended in betrayal.

When I fell in love, my heart did open up . . . but so did my intuition. At some point in the relationship, my intuition began to tell me that the man I'd fallen in love with was not telling me the truth. Although I had no tangible proof, my heart just knew it. My brain wouldn't believe it, though. And, as is the usual situation when the head and the heart are at loggerheads, nothing made sense anymore. My mind went over and over everything—I tried to deconstruct and analyze all the things we had ever said to each other or done together. I'd always been able to come to a logical conclusion about things, but now I couldn't make sense of my own life. It was driving me crazy because I *knew* the truth, but I couldn't prove it. This was a tough time because I didn't have the right foundation—the confidence in my own inner knowing—to weather the storms of life.

Physically, I was crying all the time, I was getting chronic headaches and cold sores, my stomach hurt, and my body ached. It was like my body was crying out for help and telling me that things weren't right. But my head was processing the love I'd received and telling me that love meant trusting one's partner. I wanted a family so intensely that I was doing everything in my power to keep the relationship alive—even as my heart and my body were working overtime to give me the messages I needed to hear. Since I wasn't rooted in the wisdom of my heart and intuition, however, I didn't know how to listen.

The relationship finally did end, and the agonizing and confusing time afterward was a call to do something different. What had worked for me in the past wasn't working now, and I didn't know what to do. Nothing made sense anymore. But when I shared my feelings with a good friend and told her that I couldn't bear to think that my life was going to stay this empty, hopeless, and meaningless, she recommended a holistic facilitator who would visit my house to "clear the energy" and help me feel better. At this point, I had no idea what a holistic facilitator did or what this person would do to me or my home. I didn't know what clearing energy meant, but I was open to exploring *anything* that would make me feel better and help me make sense of the world again.

The holistic facilitator arrived one cool and rainy afternoon with a small canvas bag filled with matches, incense, rice, candles, and a few other things that didn't really seem to go together. Her name was Summer, and as she walked through my home, she talked to me about what was happening in my life. She then spent some time clearing the energy using handfuls of rice, prayers, and incense. I didn't really know what was going on, but Summer had a sincere connection to the energy, and her presence alone made me feel safer. She emanated the warmth and assurance of a grandmother who only wants the best for you and is able to give you that love and appreciation with just the wink of an eye.

I soon became a regular client of Summer's, and we talked about what was happening in my life. She also taught me how to meditate and create an altar. Mine holds two candles; three cups of water; a bowl filled with rice to use for holding incense; a plant; and statues of Buddha, Guanyin, and Ganesh. I had purchased these statues on my adventures and pulled them together as I was creating my special place. They weren't idols; rather, they reminded me of my love of travel and represented the love, peace, and freedom I wanted to feel in my Life Garden.

Summer told me to sit in front of my altar and close my eyes for 15 minutes a day. This was new territory for me—after all, I'd grown up in a conservative New England household and was now living in the Deep South. No one I knew meditated or had an altar in his or her home. On the outside, it felt silly, but on the inside, it felt good to sit there and imagine all the possibilities that I wanted to create in my life. At first I had no idea what I was doing and didn't feel like anything was happening, but I continued because I trusted the process.

It turns out that the ritual of lighting the candles, filling the water cups, and lighting the incense ended up becoming a trigger for my body to enter meditation more easily. After a short time, something incredible happened: I started to feel better. For those few minutes a day in which I was sitting in a stream of pure love energy, I became so calm that I could release my pain and heal.

As I cultivated my meditation practice, my roots developed, and I learned to honor myself and trust my intuition. Through meditation, I was able to discern the difference between what other people had been telling me and what I knew was true. I also learned that my body was trying to express what my heart knew and what God was trying to tell me. Now, safe in the knowledge that I was rooted firmly in myself, the Universe, and the wisdom of my intuition, I could finally make peace with what happened and let the relationship go.

When we get quiet and still, we connect to the creative source and intelligence of the Universe, and we become rooted in something unshakable and profound. And if we meditate with the sincere intention to connect to our energy source, then we always receive spiritual assistance, even when it may feel as if nothing is happening.

Meditation is not always a happy, beautiful, serene practice of stillness and love . . . but it *is* essential. When we connect with our soul self and the Universe through this practice and allow and trust our own feelings, it makes life easier. We become more successful in offering our gifts to the world, and our journey becomes more joyful. When we get in touch with our inner being, we can release these sensitive energies and move through them, and be free to feel our best.

There are days when I don't want to meditate and feel that there isn't time, there's too much going on, or I don't have the right setting.

When I come up with such excuses, I know it means something is rising within me that wants to move on through—such as fear, a block, or some kind of emotion. That's when it's most important to sit down and examine what's really going on.

When you learn to look within, you become aware of your mind, your heart, and your soul; as well as where your thoughts really come from. This realization will help you start to find your true essence, and you may even feel your consciousness beyond your mind. Meditation doesn't have to be weird or "woo-woo," though; it's about quieting your mind so that you can get in touch with yourself and connect to a source of energy greater than all of us.

Meditation, loving yourself, and learning how to allow energy to guide you on your path can be practiced anywhere without making a lot of changes in your life. It doesn't matter where you practice— be it in nature, your living room, a church or a temple, or an empty conference room on your lunch break. (One woman I know even meditates in her closet!) All you need is a quiet place where you can still your mind.

Here is a basic meditation exercise to get you started.

Exercise: Basic Meditation

If you've never meditated before, sitting still for any amount of time can feel like an eternity, or it might even remind you of getting sent to the corner when you were a child. Yet meditation is not scary, it's not that difficult, and you don't need anything radical or special to start. In the beginning, the only thing that you need is the time to practice. So set the mood, create a sacred space, and commit to sit and quiet your mind.

At first you may want to try a guided-meditation CD, or at least memorize these steps so that you're familiar with them before you try. It's a personal journey, so check in with yourself and do what feels right for you.

You will need to find a place where you feel safe closing your eyes and won't be disturbed—it can in your home or out in nature. You may also want to bring a candle, statue, or some other item that reminds you of the energy of compassion and love in the world; along with some incense if this feels right. If you're committed to the practice, you may want to set up one sacred place so that you can return to the same spot each time you meditate. This allows the energy to accumulate, and helps you access your connection more quickly as you continue to meditate. It's also important to keep some rituals the same for every meditation: for example, candles, incense, and bowing in and out are the basic minimum. If you don't feel comfortable doing this, then come up with your own system, but this is what has worked for me.

Find 15 to 20 minutes when you won't be disturbed. (You may want to use a kitchen timer or the alarm on your cell phone when you first start so you can keep track of the time without opening your eyes.) You'll also want to wear loose-fitting clothing made of natural fibers, such as a yoga outfit or pajamas. It might be easiest to start by lying on your back, or you can try kneeling. I find that the easiest posture is cross-legged with palms up on the knees, and it's what I use.

Meditating is a very sacred opportunity to connect with yourself and the energy source of the Universe. So with that intention, try the following:

1. Light a candle and some incense.

2. Close your eyes.

3. Put your hands in a prayer position in front of your chest, then move them up to your forehead and bow down to the ground. When you come up, bring your hands to your heart. (You are bowing to your energy source, your God, or to the Universe. It is a sign of respect and acknowledges that you honor all living things. By placing your palms at your forehead and then at your heart as you bow, you are also setting the intention that you're connecting the power of your mind and heart with your spirit.)

4. Rest your hands gently on your knees with your palms open.

5. Breathe deeply into your belly.

6. Scan your body for any pain or discomfort. Notice what you feel.

7. Breathe in love, and breathe out any pain or discomfort in your body. Continue to breathe deep belly breaths until you get into a regular pattern. Try placing your hands on your belly to ensure that you're filling it with air.

8. Let your thoughts drift away. Try to empty your mind by concentrating on your breathing. If your mind gets carried away and you start thinking about what you have to do that day, say "thinking" or "breathing" in your mind. Learn to stop the stories going through your mind, the things you "have" to do, or any worries and concerns. (A racing mind is nothing abnormal—this is how our minds are all the time. We're just more aware of it when we sit quietly.)

9. Imagine roots shooting out from the base of your spine deep into the earth. As they dig deeply into the ground, imagine these roots bringing nourishment up to your heart. Then imagine that you've just stepped under a white spotlight, which is infusing your entire body with love. The light easily flows into every cell in your body, filling it with health and vitality. This love energy also flows to your heart, where it meets the nourishment from your roots. Imagine both of these energies mixing together and opening your heart.

10. When the time is up, bow out of your meditation. Put your hands in a prayer position in front of your chest, then move them up to your forehead and bow down to the ground. When you come up, put your hands to your heart area.

11. Silently say "Thank you," "Amen," or "So it is" to complete the meditation.

12. Before you open your eyes, scan your body again, making a mental note as to how you feel. Open your eyes.

When you take time each day to meditate, contemplate, become present, journal, or daydream—intentional "time-outs" of rest and openness—you feel more peaceful, energized, and connected. You need only 15 minutes per day to clear your mind, appreciate what you have, and just be. This clearing is essential to achieve inner peace and a solid root system, grounded in yourself and your faith in the Universe.

Committing to a daily meditation practice gives you the "juice" to live in the mundane world. Once you know how to control your thoughts and quiet your mind, you'll be able to look at your problems objectively. As a result, you'll be able to move through any situation with ease, peace, and lightness. You'll know that you're capable of getting through anything, no matter how devastating it may seem. Life doesn't have to be so hard.

Society has so many stressors that it's time for you to take a moment and slow down, get still, and become quiet. Maybe your mind races constantly or you have trouble sitting still. Or you're so busy that you could never imagine just sitting in a bathtub, watching a movie on TV, or being really present for a conversation with a friend.

If you're constantly on the go and filled with activity, then there's energy inside you that wants to be released. Are you so afraid that if you relax, you might "lose it"? Do you fear that you might break down and never be able to pick up the pieces? If so, know that meditation is an effective way to move through these insecure feelings. It helps clear the thoughts from your head, opens your heart, and grounds your energy so that you're more present. And it's good for your health to boot, bringing you stress reduction and increased longevity, along with a deep sense of well-being and inner peace. You may also experience better relationships, more creativity, better sleep, increased energy, and a stronger connection to your own intuition.

The reason that meditation is so powerful is that people who engage in this practice shift their brain activity from different areas of the cortex, from the stress-prone right prefrontal cortex to the calmer left prefrontal cortex. Studies have shown that meditators are healthier in all ways—physically, mentally, and emotionally—and they actually produce more "happy" chemicals, which are then released into the body. So . . . what are you waiting for?

Contrary to what you might think about meditation, you don't have to get in touch with your spiritual self by going to an ashram or hiding in a cave for a year—it's just as easy to do so while living in a city, or if you have a family and a job. All it requires is dedication, an open mind, inner work, and a desire to plant your roots deep in the soil of freedom.

Knowing ourselves means that we're rooted in just *being*. We spend so much time trying and doing, and very little time sitting with ourselves. Yet what we want is not "out there." It's inside of us. Whatever isn't happening externally is the result of an internal block. When we're honest with ourselves, then we're able to sit with ourselves—and this opens us up. Meditation is about allowing ourselves to rest, to gain control over our thoughts so that we're rooted in the truth of our divine intuition and the trust that we have all the answers inside of us. This is true freedom.

As you grow your roots deep into the earth, you'll be able to stand firmly in your own Life Garden no matter what is going on around you. And in the next chapter, we'll plant the seed of nourishment to provide the right fertilizer for your Garden to absolutely thrive.

Digging Deeper: An "Altared" Life

To dig deeper and root freedom in your life, you can:

1. Set up an altar. Create an altar in your home, a special place where you can journal, pray, meditate, and just be you. Make this space appealing and representative of what you want your garden to look like. You'll need a sturdy piece of furniture with a flat top that can hold all the elements of your garden: *earth* (a potted plant), *water* (a fountain or cups of water), *fire* (candles), *air* (incense), and *spirit* (a statue that's symbolic to you). You also want to have some space to keep important items such as a book, some photographs, or your journal. You don't want this place to become messy or too cluttered; instead, it should be a calming and beautiful area that makes you feel special and helps you root down into who you really are. Your altar is representative of your free will, and you are using it to connect to your higher self.

2. Listen to the CD in the book-and-CD set *Getting into the Vortex: Guided Meditations CD and User Guide* by Esther and Jerry Hicks. If you've never meditated, this is a good resource to help you relax, get into a state of allowing, and become aligned with your source energy. The CD has four powerful guided daily meditations for the major areas of your life: General Well-Being, Financial Abundance, Physical Well-Being, and Relationships. You can imagine your Life Garden as you listen to each meditation.

3. Commit to sit. If you truly want to root freedom into your life and are sincerely interested in changing your life, then commit to sitting in a meditation practice (listening to guided CD or meditating on your own) for at just 15 minutes each day for 21 days. If you do this, your life truly will be "altared."

CHAPTER FOUR

NOURISHMENT

"What lies behind us and what lies before us are
tiny matters compared to what lies within us."

— RALPH WALDO EMERSON

Taking care of a garden is like caring for any living thing. Plants
need clean air, water, food, rest, sunlight, and protection from the elements in order to thrive. We can apply the same principles of simple
nourishment to our own lives as well. If we want to make any type
of change, we have to give ourselves some extra attention—which
we can do by learning how to express self-love. As we love ourselves,
we demonstrate that we are worthy and enough, just as we are. And
then we're able to grow deeper roots, expand our inner strength, and
open our hearts to the magic of life.

In this book's previous chapters, we figured out what we currently
have in our Life Gardens, focused on what we want to develop, and
began to root the seeds we planted. Now, as the first green shoots
begin to appear in our Gardens, we must learn to nourish the new life
we've fostered so that it can grow into a lush and fruitful area. When

we provide nourishment for our sprouting seeds, we're supplying them with the necessities for life, health, and growth.

As you look at your particular Life Garden, you may find that you're spiritually depleted or emotionally wrung out. You may find that you're low on energy, and feel as if you've got nothing to offer the world. This is when the seed of nourishment can help you replenish the resources you need inside of yourself, in order to keep your growth active and vital.

In gardening terms, when your soil becomes depleted, it's time to give the plants a little nutrient-rich mulch (a top dressing that's created out of composted plants, fruits, vegetables, and leaves from last year's garden). Mulch not only provides the necessary nourishment for the soil, but it also has the added benefit of providing you with plenty of earthworms—the subterranean gardeners of the world—to aerate the soil and allow your root systems to breathe and stretch their fragile tendrils outward.

In today's competitive, bottom-line-driven world, life can become so busy. Our schedules are full, our minds are overstimulated, and our souls are starving for meaning and purpose. Many of us are exhausted, full of anxiety, or borderline depressed. In order to make changes in our outer Life Gardens, we first need to make changes internally by nourishing our souls. The quality and quantity of our physical, mental, emotional, and spiritual energy is directly affected by how we're caring for ourselves. If we're inadequately provided for in any of these areas, the entire landscape suffers.

Mary's Story

Mary is a client of mine who just couldn't seem to commit to self-nourishment. Outwardly, this woman projected the image of a confident, strong, successful mother of two who was happily married, well educated, and a pillar of her community. Inwardly, though, she felt alone and petrified.

After Mary's mother died, she just didn't know how to cope. Things started unraveling in her life to the point that she felt as if the world were crashing down around her. Yet the more her anxiety spiked, the busier she made herself. She tried to be constantly on the go so that she could distract herself from the growing panic at the core of her being. She also starting turning to food for comfort, becoming a secret binge eater.

Although Mary was intelligent and successful and seemed to be living the American Dream, she'd become so busy taking care of everybody else's needs that she had nothing left to share with herself. My client knew in her heart that the life she was leading wasn't sustainable, healthy, or beneficial for anyone in her family. She knew she had to slow down, admit her problem, and stop bingeing . . . but for some reason, she just couldn't. The woman was addicted.

Mary and I talked about her situation, and I suggested that she start doing something small to replenish her own resources, such as taking a sea-salt bath for 20 minutes each day. I explained that this would help her on many levels and would be a good way to quiet her mind and potentially alleviate some of her anxiety. At the very least, it would get her to slow down for a few minutes to nourish herself instead of stuffing herself with empty calories. Mary was afraid to just sit still and soak in a hot tub, however. The thought of that much quiet time, without the distractions of her hectic schedule or the comfort of her potato chips and candy bars, terrified her.

I couldn't understand what was so scary about soaking in a salt bath. But then I realized that for someone like Mary, this was probably one of the most defenseless and frightening situations imaginable. For a woman who was running away from her feelings and didn't like her body, being naked in a tub of hot water would be pretty jarring. There, she'd be shut off from distraction or external stimulation of any kind, left alone with the very thoughts and feelings she spent her whole day trying to avoid.

There would be nothing to do, nothing to hide behind—such as a job, clothes, or keeping busy with the house and kids—and nothing to distract Mary from her thoughts and emotions. She'd be floating in the water, in a vulnerable position, alone with her true self. But this is exactly what she had to do. She needed to be all alone with the thoughts and feelings that frightened her.

I knew that my client wasn't going to be able to nourish herself properly until she learned to face the fear of the stillness and get in touch with the true source of her energy, her spiritual self. Therefore, I suggested that she start slowly, trying to soak in a hot tub for just 5 minutes a day, and then gradually increase the time to 10 minutes, and then onward until she was able to sit in a tub for 20 minutes without panicking.

It took her six months, but eventually Mary was able to unwind in the bath, without anxiety, for a half hour a day, and the impact of that nourishment on her entire system allowed her to grow beyond her dependence on overachievement and then acknowledge her eating problem—and it made it easier for her to spend more quality time with herself and her family.

We all want to be loved and to know that we matter. We want to be healthy. We want to lose weight. We want to make more money. We want to be good parents. We want to enjoy our jobs. We want to be more giving and loving. So why don't we do the things we know we need to do for ourselves and for those around us? Why do we continue to drink too much, work too much, eat junk food, smoke, sit on the couch and watch TV for hours on end, and talk in an unloving way to ourselves and others?

Essentially, most of us don't make the changes we need to make because we fail to see ourselves as worthy. Yet we're all worthy of love. We *are* love. It's when we can love ourselves enough to breathe into all aspects of ourselves and accept whatever rises through us—be it fear, unworthiness, anger, or rage—that we're able to get the sustenance we need to grow.

Our tendency to nurture everybody and everything around us except for ourselves is one of the biggest threats to our freedom (particularly for us women). Yet how can we truly care for others if we don't tend to ourselves?

In addition, if we don't accept all aspects of ourselves, that's when we want to be in charge of others. Most of us try to control the people in our lives because we're unable to deal with certain parts of ourselves—we want to cut out the "bad" parts or just ignore them. We don't want to admit that we have anger, jealousy, impatience, or bitterness in our hearts.

Many of us move through our lives trying to give others the impression that we're fine, that everything is perfect, and that we have everything under control. But nobody has everything under control, and no Life Garden is pest free. We all have these so-called bad parts of the self, and if we don't accept them, then we aren't able to fully live life as a whole person. We need to accept and love *all* aspects of ourselves, whether we like those parts or not.

Many self-help books will say, "Just be happy," "Think happy thoughts," "Do things that make you happy," or "Get happy and then do your affirmations." I think these are all extremely positive things to do, but I also know that it's not the whole story. I've learned firsthand that self-nourishment can result in facing some pain, darkness, and difficulty along the way. Connecting with the inner self is not always easy, but it's always well worth it in the end.

Your foundation is developed by really loving and caring for yourself. You may think that you take pretty good care of yourself, but much of what you do is probably externally focused—daily grooming, fashion, exercising, and dieting. Real self-love is about developing a relationship with yourself. It's like dating or mothering yourself so that eventually you're able to really care about yourself without relying on another person to fulfill your needs.

If you desire more love in your life, then you need to create love in yourself first. If you desire peace in the world, then you need to create peace in yourself. If you desire truth from people, then you need to be truthful with yourself. Once you develop what you desire, then you will have created a Life Garden that will attract what you're looking for. *It all starts inside of you.*

Nourishing yourself is about loving yourself, and it's also about giving yourself whatever you need to thrive. Thus, you need to find out what that is. Just like the varieties of flora in gardens around the world, different plants need different provisions (although some combination of food, water, and care is always involved). It requires time and attention to discover what makes you and your Life Garden bloom individually, but all gardens and all people basically need some combination of the following elements in order to prosper: *water, food, movement, love,* and *rest.*

In order to help you understand the nourishment that your garden needs, let's talk about each of these elements individually.

The Power of Water

One of the simplest forms of nourishment is ensuring that we drink enough water. Water is essential for life, giving us the power to cleanse, purify, sustain, and renew our bodies. When we're hydrated, we're calmer, our energy is balanced, and we just feel better overall. Many religions acknowledge the spiritually healing and cleansing properties of water. It's also nothing short of the fundamental source of all life on this planet—we can live for weeks without food, but without water, we'd wither and die in just a few days.

For most of us, water flows effortlessly from our faucets. We think little about the journey it makes from its source to our homes, not concerning ourselves with the daily obstacles it must overcome to wind up in our glasses or bottles. There are many, however, for whom water is scarce, and a constant struggle to secure. An eighth of the world's population doesn't have access to clean drinking water, and more than 3.5 million people, mostly children, die from water-related diseases each year. As the supply dwindles even more, it may come to be seen as more precious than petroleum.

If water were as scarce for the rest of us, however, perhaps we would respect and value it more. Yet those of us who are lucky enough to have ready and constant access to pure fresh water have come to take this precious resource for granted. We allow our businesses to poison our lifeblood with chemicals, trash, and other pollutants. We dam it up, thus destroying the ecology of our lakes, rivers, and streams in the process. We let oil slicks strangle our oceans. We treat water with disrespect and forget to take advantage of the many blessings and miracles it can bring us—if only we'd just engage with it and revere it, giving it a place of honor in our lives each and every day.

Water has many incredible properties that are hidden in the intangible realms because it is a conductor of energy. Its vibration and memory are programmed by the environment; it has the power to transmit life, death, and miracles. Water has electromagnetic and chemical properties that allow it to absorb energy vibrations that are impressed upon it by the environment, similar to the way a magnetic tape records the sound of the voice. Water is an ongoing exchange of energy and information between our bodies and the environment around us.

Dr. Masaru Emoto, a Japanese researcher, proved what I'm talking about here when he published incredible photographs of water and the information it carries. In his book *The Hidden Messages in Water*, Dr. Emoto explains the results of his fascinating experiments with water crystals. He collected samples of water from different sources, labeled the bottles with positive messages such as "I love you," "Gratitude," and "Appreciation"; or negative messages such as "I hate you," "You fool," and "I will kill you." He then froze droplets from each of the bottles and examined them using Magnetic Resonance Analysis technology.

He found that water changed its molecular structure to match the influences in its environment: positive words, prayers, and classical music produced perfectly clear, symmetrical crystals; while what resulted from negative words, angry thoughts, and discordant or jarring music were disfigured, discolored, and asymmetrical crystals. (To see these photos, go to Dr. Emoto's website: **www.masaru-emoto.net**.)

So if thoughts can do that to mere droplets, and we're made up of 75 percent water, what might our thoughts be doing to our bodies?

If we want to nourish ourselves, we need to drink at least eight to ten glasses of water per day. Keeping ourselves hydrated plays a significant role in reducing the risk of many diseases, and it helps keep our skin clear and our muscles toned. Water transports oxygen and nutrients to our bodies' cells, and it also eliminates the toxins and wastes from those cells. In addition, it helps us lose weight and regulate body temperature as well as blood pressure. There probably isn't a more universally beneficial tonic in the world than water.

Another way to benefit from this nourishing element is to take a sea-salt bath. Saltwater soaks have historically been known to be effective treatments for rejuvenating the cells and creating a healthy exchange of minerals and toxins between the blood and the water. People have traveled the world to bathe in the Dead Sea due to its therapeutic properties; Cleopatra and the Queen of Sheba used sea salt for its unique abilities to relax the mind, nourish and smooth the skin, and soothe the soul; and Hippocrates encouraged patients to bathe in salt water in ancient times.

Salt has many benefits: an improved immune system; increased circulation; rejuvenated cells; and moist, clear skin. Salt also has minerals that restore the body's mineral balance, and establishes a proper balance of alkaline and acid throughout the whole system. It relieves tension, relaxes your body, and rejuvenates your mind. Consequently, taking a sea-salt bath increases your vitality, decreases your stress, and improves your quality of sleep. It can also can help you be more positive, increase your self-confidence, create a better relationship with yourself, and give you peace of mind.

In other words, if you're feeling cranky, stuck in your thinking, tired, achy, or just plain bogged down by life, drink a glass of water or soak in a sea-salt bath for 20 minutes. It's guaranteed to put the spring back in your step, flush out your body, and restore your balance.

The Fuel of Food

As a child, my family always had fresh fruits and vegetables around. If it wasn't from our own garden (or my grandfather's), we purchased it from a local farmer who put up a stand in the summertime.

We grew the basics in our garden: tomatoes, peppers, carrots, cucumbers, and an occasional watermelon or squash. We also had raspberries, blackberries, strawberries, and blueberries—which I'd often pick right off the bush. We didn't think of purchasing our produce from the local Stop & Shop. We knew where our food came from, and it was delicious.

In today's mass-produced, sliced, diced, packaged, and shipped world, we've forgotten what food is like in its natural state . . . and many of us have no idea where it comes from at all. We've traded the feeling of being nourished from, and connected with, the earth through our food—all for the convenience of take-out and prepared meals. Food has become something we grab on the run, shovel down in a hurry, or get "to go." And we rarely make healthy choices about how to nourish ourselves when we're so rushed. How many of us cook from scratch anymore? Who has time for that? Yet in order to get the proper nourishment and reconnect with our energy source, food should be slow, not fast; and fresh, not processed.

In this land of plenty, it's easy to forget that hunger is a huge problem in the world. There are an estimated 925 million people around the globe who are undernourished. Therefore, we should always try to be appreciative and respectful of the food we eat. This means thinking about *what* we're eating, knowing where it comes from, understanding how it grows, and becoming familiar with the gardens that grew it. Honoring our food is about growing our own— or at least shopping at farmers' markets—and creating delicious meals out of what is whole, organic, and locally available. We can also honor our food by *giving thanks* for the food that we put in our bodies and *enjoying* our food and eating until we're satisfied. It's not about stuffing ourselves with empty calories so that when we're done, we're full but deeply unsatisfied.

Know that you are always able to heal yourself and transform the way you look and feel through the food you eat. And you don't have to make a lot of changes at one time. I like what health and wellness expert Kathy Freston says about "leaning" into a new routine. You don't have to try to break a lifetime of habits at once or throw everything out of your pantry. Instead, simply move in that direction and make small changes. Those small changes add up to bigger changes; eventually, you'll shift your vibration surrounding food altogether.

If everything has energy, then the food you eat comes with it, too. So what kind of energy do you want to put in your body? Your food can either be a life enhancer and bring you vitality, or it can be a toxic death trap stripped of all its goodness.

I've personally become very aware that the big manufacturers that supply so many items we eat see it as a business instead of as sustenance. I'm also mindful of how food can nourish my body, so I've become much more careful about what I purchase. I look at where the item comes from, what's added to it, and how I feel about it; I've also chosen to cook meals at home and limit my meat, dairy, and processed-food intake. And I go to the farmers' market when I can, buy organic, and make my own yogurt at home. I'm leaning into these changes and am noticing how my body reacts to them. I don't always make the right decision, but I'm doing my best to make choices that are delicious, nutritious, and nourishing for my body.

Megan Wooden's Story

I met Megan on a Hay House cruise to Alaska in the summer of 2009. She was a beautiful and poised woman in her mid-30s who reminded me of a younger Priscilla Presley; she also came across as intelligent, kind, and very healthy. I noticed that she didn't drink alcohol, was very particular about the food she ate, and made sure that she got her exercise and sleep during the cruise. I was impressed by how balanced she seemed about everything, so I asked her a few questions about her lifestyle. What I found out amazed me, and proved that there is always more to a person than meets the eye.

Megan had experienced several significant challenges over the years, but instead of being a victim, she decided to take control of her life and overcome those challenges by balancing out her health and wellness. It turns out that at the age of 28—and ten days before her daughter's second birthday—Megan was confronted with the words, "You have cancer." She had stage III melanoma, which meant that the disease had traveled from its original site to one of her lymph nodes. Fortunately, there was only a very small amount of cancer in the lymph node, so Megan and her doctors thought that they'd caught it before it was able to spread. That's what they believed for another three and a half years . . . until she found a lump while doing a routine breast exam in the shower.

This time the discovery came just one week before her wedding to the man of her dreams. So instead of getting caught up in all the doctors' visits and so forth, Megan and her future husband decided to go forward with their wedding plans. A month later she learned that the original melanoma had metastasized, spreading to both her breast and lung.

At just 31 years old with four children—a daughter from a previous marriage and three from her new husband's previous marriage—Megan was diagnosed with stage IV metastatic melanoma and was told she would only have a year to live. Yet she decided that "dying was not an option" for her.

Megan made the conscious decision to research and try everything to overcome this health challenge. She decided to focus on her inner world to see if she could change her outer world. She started running to relieve stress, and ran her first full marathon with tumors in her lung. She also started integrating many nontraditional treatments and nutritional, emotional, and lifestyle changes into her life. These included many of the things discussed in this book: a positive outlook, affirmations, meditation, exercise, healthy eating, self-care, connecting deeply with other people, letting go, deep breathing, acupuncture, and laughter. Thanks to this rigorous treatment and her will to live, Megan's tumors miraculously dissolved.

Now, more than five years after receiving her "terminal" diagnosis with only a one percent chance of living five years, there is no evidence of cancer in Megan's body. She lives in Salt Lake City, Utah, with her husband and children and speaks about the power of "soaring above" when faced with a life challenge. She is a much stronger person physically, emotionally, and spiritually because of what she has gone through. Her case is truly miraculous and demonstrative of the power to heal.

Megan realized that by balancing out all aspects of her life, she was not only able to gain a new perspective, but a new life altogether. She changed her inner world—what she ate, what she thought, whom she associated with, and how she perceived things. All that, in turn, changed her outer world—her cancer, her relationships, and her well-being. She now lives a life of freedom and infinite possibilities, and continues to focus on her health and wellness.

The Freedom of Movement

I've always been athletic, but I often associated exercise with guilt. It was something I did to lose weight, so I was either very active (exercising every day) or not doing anything at all. But as I connected with myself on a deeper level and realized that moving my body was a way to connect to myself mentally, physically, and spiritually, I saw exercise in a whole new light. I started to ask my body what it wanted—and I listened. I knew when I needed to stretch, go for a run, do some strength training, or take a rest and do nothing. It wasn't about following a regimen no matter what or pushing through the pain. Movement became something I did with my body that made me feel good and enriched my life.

When we move with joy, we're connected to our bodies and can attune to our inner wisdom. We can then clear our field, loosen the soil so our roots can grow deeper, and break up the boulders in life. Movement gives us vitality, a sound mind, and a clear spirit.

Keep in mind that we were built to move—we weren't created to sit behind a desk, sit on a sofa watching television, or play on the computer. To that end, the Centers for Disease Control (CDC) recommends at least 30 minutes of exercise five times a week to reap its benefits, such as an increased sense of happiness, improved health, and better quality of sleep. But for many of us who lead incredibly busy lives, exercise can sometimes feel like a chore. It becomes a task we have to check off a list if we want to keep our body looking a certain way. We see Oprah herself clearly expressing her dislike for exercise as she continues to struggle with her weight in such a public forum, and we can surely relate.

Exercise the way we know it today—strenuous aerobic activity and pumping iron—is a very "doing" type of activity. It has a strong masculine energy and is about strength, competition, and external power. Sometimes this isn't what we need, though. It doesn't mean that we become coach potatoes for the rest of our days, but it might mean that we need to take a break and use that time to bring some softer energies and feminine forms of movement into our lives.

Dana Brownlee's Story

Dana and I went to business school together. She was always in the front row asking questions, offering answers and insights, and basically taking the world by storm. She was also beautiful and always seemed to have a boyfriend. We weren't really friends back then, but after we both left our corporate jobs and started our own businesses, we reconnected to talk about working together in some way. At this point, she didn't have a boyfriend and had decided to concentrate on herself. What I loved was that in addition to starting her consulting business, she was taking dancing lessons as well as scheduling private Pilates classes a few times a week. She looked fabulous.

What's more, Dana was having fun, not just out looking for a guy. And she was connecting with her body through Pilates, yoga, and the meringue—she wasn't punishing it with lots of running on the unforgiving pavement or endless reps on a machine at the gym. Dana nourished herself with movement and did what was right for her body while she transitioned from one man to the other. She didn't fill up on food or just sit at home and watch TV. She got out, met people, and moved her body. Not only did all of this make her look amazing, but it also shifted her energy, too. Ultimately, she ended up meeting her husband, Shaun.

Dana continues to make movement a priority as she balances her business consulting, her speaking engagements around the world, her relationships with Shaun and their two-year-old baby girl, and her community service. She still likes to go out dancing with her husband, take a Pilates class, or quiet her mind through yoga. Dana is inspiring in the way she's able to care for herself, connect with her body, and gain some much-needed freedom through movement.

When you move your body, you can feel your heart pumping, and you know you're alive! So move your body—shake it, wiggle it, or twirl it. Find out what moves you, what makes your body feel full of energy and enthusiasm, and do that. It might be that you go outside for a walk with your dogs, or ride your bike or grab your hula hoop. You can take up dancing like Dana; or try yoga, hiking, or swimming. But find *something* that makes you feel good, is good for your body, and doesn't feel like a chore—something that motivates you to move your body and makes you feel free!

Love and Kindness

Every human being needs love to survive, but we can't offer or receive it until we're able to love ourselves. First and foremost, loving ourselves means being kind—through our thoughts and words, the types of activities we do for ourselves, and the way we treat others. We also experience kindness in a sweet voice, a tender touch, or the twinkle of an eye. When kindness becomes a way of life, we're gentler, more sympathetic, and more present in the moment; we're also more spiritually satisfied because we're in a stream of love energy.

Most of us don't realize how unkind we are to ourselves. We complain about everything in our Life Gardens—and in the process, we're not allowing the seeds we've planted to grow because the Gardens aren't getting the proper nourishment. Just being ourselves should be enough—when we're kind to ourselves, then we know we *are* enough in whatever we're doing.

When we can bring this kindness to ourselves and others, then we can give ourselves a break. We might celebrate our small successes and be more sweet and nurturing when things don't always go our way. It might help to think of ourselves as tiny seedlings with delicate roots that are tentatively breaking the soil of new ground. We wouldn't yell at the seedlings, yank them up, or expect them to be healthy and strong on day one. Rather, we'd give them encouragement and celebrate the successes of incremental growth. We'd see how fragile they are. When we're in "deep change," or the process of emerging from a seed to a green sprout, we're fragile as well and need the same gentle touch.

Just like we do for our babies, we have to be the mother to the child inside our hearts and take special care with respect to the thoughts we think in our mind (inner dialogue, self-confidence); the words we say about ourselves (self-talk, accepting compliments); the actions we take to show ourselves love (lotions, potions, clothes, rituals); and the way we care for ourselves (sleep, rest, food, getting outside, water). If we aren't kind and gentle to ourselves, who will be? As we mother our inner child, we learn to come into our wholeness.

No matter what happens externally in our lives—a breakup, a layoff, loss of money, a family drama, an unfulfilling job, or a health problem—we cannot lose our love for ourselves. When we're kind to ourselves, our energy is continually fed from within, allowing us the freedom to move on to the next phase of our development. We feel loved, trusted, and properly nourished from the inside out.

Rest Is the Best

Rest allows your body to restore and renew itself, and it also brings you to a place of stillness so that you can connect with your higher self. While you're sleeping, your mind, body, and spirit are hard at work repairing and getting ready for the next day. Sleep triggers important hormones that fight infection and stimulate your metabolism, helps you think clearly and react quickly, and builds memory. Lack of sleep is linked to negative physical and emotional health: people who don't sleep enough have higher levels of inflammation and fasting insulin; they also have other risks, such as increased risk of diabetes and heart disease, and they're more apt to be depressed or angry.

As I began to root deeply in my Life Garden, I noticed that my need for sleep increased. Note that planting your own Life Garden and doing the internal work is a strenuous activity and may require additional rest. When you view sleeping as an essential element in your self-care, then it becomes a priority and is nonnegotiable. Whenever you sacrifice your slumber in order to please someone else or get more done in a day, you're actually depleting your reserves and not allowing yourself to rejuvenate. In fact, you're stealing time from the future because lack of sleep doesn't allow you to experience life in the moment, which ultimately impairs your growth in the Garden.

Sleep is easy nourishment for your body, so feather your nest with things that make you feel wonderful (new sheets, down comforters, scented sprays, or the like); don't watch TV right before you go to sleep; avoid caffeine, nicotine, and alcohol before bedtime; get plenty of exercise; and wake up with the sun. And as you're falling asleep each night, appreciate all the good in your Life Garden, relax into a state of goodness, and ask your spirit to assist you as you drift off. If you fall asleep in your dream Garden, then you'll wake up there as well.

This practice of feeling good and then falling asleep for seven to nine hours is an important part of taking care of your mind, body, and soul. Sleep is an absolutely critical element in the nourishment of your Life Garden.

Exercise: **Make Your Life Delicious**

For the next 30 days, consciously do one thing to nourish yourself. This is not about being perfect; it's about making your life genuinely delicious. Choose one thing you can do each day and, as you're doing it, make it as gentle and loving as you can.

Here are five things I nourish myself with that you might enjoy, too:

1. Water. Fill a pitcher equal to eight glasses of water and pop in a few fresh strawberries, which will infuse the water with a fresh taste. (You can also use limes, lemons, pineapple, or oranges.) I put a pitcher on my desk at work so I have something beautiful to look at and know how much water I've consumed during the day. You can also bless the water with positive energy for an additional boost of nourishment.

2. Food. Take a day to eat only fresh fruits and vegetables. Pay attention to the "life" that is still in the food to note if it's something you want to put in your body. Also, pay attention to how you feel when you eat fresher foods. I do a raw-food cleanse once a month—on those days, I either take my food with me or plan to eat at restaurants that serve fresh, organic foods and juices.

3. Movement. Find a local hiking trail or botanical garden and go for a one-hour walk without any music, keeping your phone on silent. It's important to get out and walk by yourself in nature to get your body moving and connect with the sounds and beauty of your environment. I go for walks in nature at least three times a week, and good ideas and insights tend to come to me when I do so.

4. Self-love. In my wallet, I carry a picture of myself as a small child. It reminds me to be kind to myself.

5. Rest. Put on fresh sheets on your bed, turn off the television, and go to sleep early—all of which will help you get eight full hours of interrupted rest. I value my sleep over most things these days, and find that by getting enough, I feel more vibrant and alive during the day.

These are all loving acts that you can do for yourself on a daily basis. What five things are you going to add to your life? Write your responses in your journal or notebook.

1. Water:

2. Food:

3. Movement:

4. Self-love:

5. Rest:

All of these self-care rituals work together to support your well-being—emotionally, physically, mentally, and spiritually. As you start to nourish yourself with the ingredients that are essential for your growth, you will feel your center of personal power and your ability to create strengthen. As you nourish and love yourself, you'll start to feel more energized, powerful, and ready for action. Your self-image will change, and you'll have a stronger sense of self that comes from within, not from the external and fleeting things in life.

It takes courage to connect with and nourish all aspects of who you are. It's not always comfortable, and it's certainly not always easy. When you truly take care of yourself, you connect to those sensitive and vulnerable areas that many people don't explore. And some individuals in your life may not understand what you're doing. Not everyone will like or approve of the changes you're making, and that's okay. The important thing is that you feel happy, nourished, and strong enough to support yourself during stormy times and droughts, as well as through periods of transformation and growth.

When you give yourself nourishment physically, emotionally, and spiritually, you're presenting yourself with love. You're rooting in your own Life Garden. These roots can pull up the necessary nutrition, nurturing, and nourishment you need to live a fulfilling life. Then you'll have the energy to help other people as well—and you'll be able to access your inner power, open your heart, and continue to grow in the direction of a fully accessible and free expression of yourself in the world. This is true freedom.

Next, we're going to plant the seed of growth.

Digging Deeper: Extreme Self-Care

To dig deeper and learn how to really nourish your Life Garden, you can:

1. Read *The Art of Extreme Self-Care* by Cheryl Richardson. In this easy-to-read and insightful book, Cheryl provides 12 monthly lessons to transform your life by helping you really care for yourself. Each lesson is designed to help you put an end to the endless cycle of self-betrayal and neglect.

2. Take a sea-salt bath. If you can't find the time to soak quietly in a tub for 20 minutes, there's something deeper going on in your life that needs to be addressed. Make a concerted effort to draw a bath, light a candle, and throw in a handful of sea salt into the tub. Then step in, relax into the water, close your eyes, and go through all your senses. Really feel the water, and then visualize the negative energy leaving your body along with your cares and woes. Roll over onto your tummy. Dunk your head. How do you feel in the bath? Be with your thoughts. . . .

This soak is not about cleansing your body per se. A sea-salt bath allows your nervous system to relax and unwind; it allows the tension in your body to dissolve along with your worries. If you step into the tub to unwind and really allow yourself to relax, you can imagine that the water is giving you a big hug and filling your body with love, warmth, and nourishment.

3. Write a love list. Write down all the things you love about yourself. You can keep this ongoing list in your journal, but really start to notice all the good things about yourself. At work, it can be that you make the first pot of coffee in the morning, you always share your chocolate, or you're unfailingly punctual for meetings. At home, it might be that you're a good spouse or parent, you shovel your neighbor's driveway, you help out in your kid's classroom, you cheer on the soccer team, or you smile at people at the mall. Perhaps you're kind to animals, you're a good listener, you love to laugh, or you're a passionate singer. The more you love and appreciate who you are, the more you'll really start to love and nourish yourself . . . and then you'll allow the things that you want in your Life Garden to flourish.

CHAPTER FIVE

GROWTH

"And the day came when the risk to
remain tight in a bud was more painful
than the risk it took to blossom."

— A N A ï s N i n

Human beings have an innate aversion to pain, and if we can find
a comfortable way to do something, we naturally choose to do so.
We certainly don't want to voluntarily venture out into a difficult or
unfamiliar situation that requires growth—in fact, most of us design
our lives specifically so that we can avoid this altogether. We stay too
busy to learn new things, we're caught in our belief patterns, or we
just never seem to find the time to reach beyond our present level.
We're happy right where we are. Or are we?

Since change is the only constant in life, growth really isn't op-
tional. As hard as we may try to keep things the same, nature will find
a way to alter them. And then we must expand in order to adapt. Yet
this is not bad news. Freedom comes from doing and learning and
trying new things.

Growth is something that takes us beyond where we are. It's about expanding our awareness and creativity, and going beyond where we thought we could go. In business, we're often told that growth is about never-ending resources and consumption, along with power and control; however, it most assuredly isn't about achievement, checking off tasks on a to-do list, or accumulating the most of anything. Real growth is about expanding our minds, hearts, and possibilities. It's about the exchange, evolution, renewal, and cycle of life.

As you start to change shape from a seed to a plant, you'll also be changing your looks and your view of the world. You'll also become vulnerable to different kinds of pests, even as you're constantly moving in the direction of your life purpose. Yes, the process of evolution can be difficult, but in order to expand your existence and create the Garden you've envisioned for yourself, you've got to move out of your comfort zone and trust that you're on the right path.

As you start to expand, it's almost guaranteed to hurt on some level (physically, mentally, or emotionally), and you may think that all the work you're doing internally isn't worth it. But once you trust that the world is a safe and spiritual place, then you can open up your energy field. Also, since whatever you put your attention on will grow strong, you need to make sure that you're focusing your energy on what you want versus what you don't want.

As you bring higher dimensions of consciousness into your awareness, then you'll start to see your surroundings in new ways, expand your thinking, and uncover new possibilities and potential in your life. You'll grow in a multidimensional way—in your thinking, interactions, and communications with the world—as you get new responses from people and things around you, even if they aren't positive. You can then label yourself as a victim or someone with bad luck, or you can see every interaction as an opportunity for growth and appreciate it. It's up to you.

Interaction with life causes things to move—and this movement shifts and shapes how we're going to grow. It's our ability to choose what makes us feel good that eventually leads us to the place where we're liberated, flourishing, and joyful. So we all need to break through the conformity of existence and declare our freedom. We must give ourselves permission to express our truth and follow our hearts. It's imperative that we learn to take care of ourselves first, dream bigger dreams, say *no* more often, and stop being so polite just for the sake of being polite. Of course, I'm not advocating that we be rude or hurtful to other people, but we do need to start being honest with ourselves instead of trying so hard to please others.

When you declare your freedom and do something aligned with your heart, then it alters the world around you. People respond differently to you, things you need show up, and you're given new situations to experience. So now is the time to take action and make some real changes. You need to announce your life vision to the world and begin expressing what you genuinely want. Put your thoughts into action by digging down deep into your soul and inviting growth into your life. The time has come for something new!

Tap into the Power of the Heart and the Field

When we feel as if we have no options, what choice do we have than to keep doing what we've been doing? What if we're out of money, need further education, or really love the person we're in a toxic relationship with and can't imagine leaving? What if we're in an unfulfilling job but are too frightened to leave it because of an economic downturn? What if we have an amazing idea but are scared of failure? How do we effect change in our garden, then? We can do so by tapping into the power of the heart and the field.

Physically, the heart is only about the size of a fist and weighs less than ten ounces, but it is no ordinary organ. The heart is responsible for pumping oxygenated and nutrient-rich blood through our bodies—it beats approximately 75 times per minute or about 40 million times per year, which adds up to more than 2.76 billion times in a 70-year lifetime! Despite its diminutive size, it's clear just how powerful this organ can be.

Today's science is proving the impact the heart has when it comes to determining our destiny and healing our bodies. To that end, the

Institute of HeartMath and the Institute of Noetic Sciences have recently discovered that the heart has an incredible intelligence, which generates significant power over the rest of the body. HeartMath's research has also shown that the heart gives off an electrical field 60 times greater in amplitude than the brain's, and a magnetic field 5,000 times greater than the brain's, making it the largest electromagnetic field in the body.

The heart's electromagnetic field contains information and coding that is transmitted inside and outside the body, and it's believed to be connected to the field of energy that connects all things in the Universe. So, although our thoughts are very mighty, our thoughts plus heart-centered intention and feeling is exponentially more powerful. Why wouldn't we want to live a life based from our heart?

The Institute of HeartMath found that heart-based emotion does, in fact, influence the magnetic fields of the earth; in addition, it helps us connect to our body's wisdom, our intuition, and our overall vitality. When we practice heart-centered techniques such as meditation, intentional breathing, and positive visualization, we can create emotional balance in our lives. These techniques reduce stress and help us develop the necessary skills to easily deal with the challenges of daily life.

Our thoughts and emotions both have a powerful influence over our own lives and the world around us. Research has shown that both the brain and the heart are electrical devices, so it's not inconceivable that when the combined thoughts and feelings of the entire world are focused on one event, they can impact all kinds of electrical fields— including those of human beings and even the planet itself. In fact, science has proven exactly that!

It turns out that the Global Consciousness Project continually collects data from 65 or 70 sites around the world from a network of physical random number generators (RNGs). Although the RNGs usually produce a string of completely random numbers, the numbers tend to correlate during major global events that evoke millions of shared intentions and emotions. For example, after the terrorist attacks on the World Trade Center in New York City on September 11, 2001, there was an initial spike in the data, and this elevated spike continued throughout the day. The researchers on this project believe that the data produced by the RNGs could suggest an interconnected web of global consciousness.

Since whatever we put our attention on grows, whenever we put our hearts into something, we're able to magnify the power of our efforts. As we focus on the vision of our Life Gardens, we can use the power of the heart to feel how we want to feel. This internal shift of feeling something before it manifests is what will bring about the Gardens of our dreams, regardless of our circumstances.

It's important to take the time to focus on the sensations of your ideal Life Garden. When you can taste, smell, see, hear, and touch what you want with the power of your heart—be it a lover, a fulfilling job, a healthy body, abundance, security, or whatever it may be—then it must come to you. The power to focus internally on feeling first instead of performing an action is powerful and profound. As you connect with your heart, life will start to bloom in ways you never imagined . . . the power of love can transform even a prison cell into a paradise.

Release Control

All gardeners trust that, in general, things want to grow. Gardeners always go about their business with optimism and do the best they can to optimize a plant's potential, but they know that they can't force a flower to bloom. We have to take a lesson from gardeners and just let growth happen, without trying to control it. We must have faith that the Universe will always take care of us.

It takes courage to rely on our inner voice and surrender. When we get out of the way and let go, it can be extremely frightening. It's like riding a roller coaster: We can either try to hold on tight and get jostled around, or we can relax and let out a *"Wheeeeeeee!"* as we let the thrill take over. It might still be scary, but it's more fun when we relax and go with the flow. And since we're going to be on the ride regardless, we may as well enjoy it.

So, take ownership of your Life Garden as much as you can, but know that you're co-creating that Garden in harmony with the Universe. As you unleash fear, you release control and accept love back into your heart. I'm sure this is going to be a tall order for many of you. (I know it was difficult for me. I had a hard time admitting that I was something of a control freak, even as I caught myself saying things like, "I like things the way I like them," or "I can do it better than anybody else.") But let me ask you, where did you get the idea you were a more competent manager than the Universe? Do you have all the answers? Do you *want to* have all the answers? And isn't it exhausting trying to control every second of every day, when you could be just relaxing and flowing along with your life's current?

The first step in letting go is to become aware of what you're holding on to. Once you find yourself stepping in to take control of things that you really can't control, come up with a mantra to recite that will remind you to take a step back. I usually tell myself something like, *Everything will turn out just fine,* or *The Universe can handle this better than I can.* Having your own mantra will help release you from feeling as if you always have to be in the driver's seat—and it will shift your energy into a more accepting, heart-centered place, too.

It's also important to try to understand what you can and can't manage in your life. You may be learning that you can be in charge of yourself—that is, your thoughts, beliefs, intentions, actions, and even physical health. You can also control your breathing, where you focus your energy, and the thoughts you think. But there are many things you *can't* control, such as other people's choices or the cycles of nature. Think about this: You can only hold a beach ball under water for so long. When you tire of applying the pressure, or switch your attention away for even a moment, that ball will pop back up to the surface each and every time. Trying to control the uncontrollable is wasted energy that could be better spent on the growth you must achieve in order to bear fruit.

When we accept where we are and understand the difference between what we can and can't control, then we'll just naturally allow the Universe to work its magic in our lives. We are never given more than what we're ready for; change will come as quickly or as slowly as we can handle. Once we know that we'll never get more than we can deal with, we can relax into the process of life and allow ourselves to live joyfully in alignment with our heart, nature, and the Universe. This one shift in perception—from doing to being—is huge when it comes to how we feel about our lives. Surrendering to the Universe brings a remarkable sense of freedom.

Just like in nature, we have to trust the flow of the growing season. We must always be open to new beginnings, fresh blooms, and unexpected surprises—a bird that makes a nest in a nearby tree, the flowers that pop up from seeds that were blown in from a neighbor's garden, or the bees that pollinate the blooms in the spring. Although we didn't plant these things ourselves, when we allow them to be a part of our landscape, we're all the better for it.

To the Universe, every moment is the start of the next big thing in your life. When you allow such wisdom to enter your world, then you're inviting possibilities and potential into your Life Garden. It seems counterintuitive, but when you allow, you loosen your grip and let the Universe help you. When you let go of the controls, you become free—free to trust, free to follow your heart, and free to grow.

JoAnn's Story

At first glance, JoAnn is a globe-trotting executive with one of the world's most renowned advertising agencies (although she happens to possess an unassuming and genuine demeanor). As executive vice president of all North American client research, analytics, and modeling, JoAnn is an expert in evaluating consumer insights for her clients across many different cultures and industries. Evaluating her own life, however, has been a greater challenge.

JoAnn's rewarding career has spanned more than 20 years in marketing, analytics, and research. Her entire life has been marked by achievement: a driven and intelligent Michigan native, she earned her undergraduate degree at Michigan State University before going on to complete an MBA, graduating Phi Beta Kappa from the Goizueta Business School at Emory University while working full-time.

But her seemingly boundless energy began to wane as her responsibilities and expectations continued to grow exponentially. Her life had become very unbalanced, as her schedule was filled with work weeks of 70 hours or more; constant travel; all-day meetings; and catching up on work whenever she wasn't in the office. She was no longer finding the time to nourish her inner self, and she finally reached a point when she knew something had to change.

JoAnn took a hard-earned 90-day sabbatical from her work to reflect and reenergize her mind, body, and spirit. She made an inventory of what she was responsible for doing daily, both in her work and in her personal life, and she realized that she was spending a lot of time on things she didn't like instead of those that brought her joy.

Much of her time on the job was spent dealing with time-consuming tasks that weren't very innovative or interesting at this stage of her career. Much of this work was also extremely time sensitive, which kept her in a reactive mode and freed up little time for creating innovative, analytical solutions or strategic, value-added work. Her home life also suffered, and she wasn't regularly engaging in those activities that brought her joy and peace—such as time with her husband, yoga, and horseback riding.

This overloaded professional decided to reprioritize her work activities by letting go of those responsibilities that were no longer fulfilling and concentrating on the ones that added real value to her clients. She also sought greater opportunities for intellectual growth to revive herself mentally, spiritually, and emotionally. Because JoAnn reallocated her time and redefined her boundaries, she is now able to focus on the most rewarding and fulfilling aspects of her profession—and, in the process, make her clients more successful. By giving up control, she's not only allowing others to grow, but she's also learning to trust her own intuition and innate wisdom.

Personally, JoAnn is cultivating the activities she truly enjoys. For example, she has a standing date with her husband every week, as well as a standing date with *herself* to get needed rest without her BlackBerry at her bedside each night. She's also made a concerted effort to manage her health. She converted to a strictly vegan lifestyle and made exercise a priority, which has increased her energy and stamina. Even when there is still work to be done, she no longer sacrifices her need for mental and physical rejuvenation through yoga or horseback riding. After all, the work will always be there.

JoAnn's definition of success does not consist of a particular title or level of economic achievement or power; rather, she is committed to living her life with faith and authenticity, both personally and professionally. As long as she remains true to herself and committed to a noble purpose, she continues to grow and expand in all aspects of her Life Garden—and *that* is her definition of success.

From Conformity to Individuality

It's time to make a bold declaration in your new Garden. It's time to break free of conformity and grow into your own sense of individuality.

It's time to move out of your head and into your heart. You may think that you know what you want—what you feel obligated to do, what your boss/mom/kids/spouse/friends want you to do, or what the media has insisted you want—but is that *really* what you want? Take action and allow some new experiences to come into your life. If you don't, then you're never going to know what you truly prefer.

Looking back, it took a lot of courage to start living life on my terms, to make decisions that weren't necessarily preserving the status quo. But it's those decisions that have made me stronger. As I was starting to cultivate a Life Garden that looked completely different from anyone else's, I kept the vision in my mind of the violets that had started me on my journey. Those violets connected me to my roots, to my lineage, and they also kept me inspired to continue to cultivate the seeds of freedom despite what others said. Those little tender and sweet flowers kept a smile on my face because I kept thinking, *If they can break through the ground against all odds, then why can't I?*

Allowing new things into our lives and moving out of our comfort zone can be awkward, uncomfortable, and messy. So we need to be lighthearted as we do so and know that it's not always going to turn out perfectly. That's okay.

As you go into this next exercise, I'd like you to approach it as if you can't fail, it's a game, and you're tasting new experiences in the buffet of life. As you try out things that you think you want or don't want, you're going to challenge your beliefs in your head . . . and see how these new experiences and beliefs feel in your heart.

Exercise: The Belief Challenge

Come up with three to five things in each area of your Life Garden that you can do to support your new vision. It can either be something that challenges a belief you currently have or something that will help move you into the feeling that your new garden is already in full bloom. I've listed a couple of examples for each element that we explored at the beginning of the book, and then I'd like you to write down your own in your journal. Have fun and see what happens!

---

1. *Earth:* Security

As you look at your Life Garden plan, what seeds have you planted for your security that you want to see grow—home, money, abundance? What can you do to tap into the power of your heart and loosen control in this area? For each of your actions, pay close attention to how it makes you feel. Do you like it? Is it what you expected? Do you like the people? What happened? How did others react?

— If you're lacking money at the moment, then for one week pretend that you're rich beyond your wildest dreams. Go shopping online, but don't actually buy anything; contact a Realtor to view a house in a neighborhood where you'd love to live; test-drive the car you've been fantasizing about; and visit the stores where you wish you could afford to shop. You don't have to spend any money, but imagine that you have spent some, and see how you feel in this new world.

— Say *no* to someone in your family and see what happens. Place boundaries around things that feel right for you, and tell that person what you're willing to do on your terms.

2. *Water:* Health and Well-being

As you look at your Life Garden plan, what seeds have you planted for your health and well-being that you want to see grow—your fitness, emotional balance, vitality? What can you do to tap into the power of your heart and let go of your need to control in this area? How does it make you feel?

— How are you currently eating? For one day, eat the way you've envisioned in your Garden and see how you feel. Now compare that with the way you feel with your typical diet.

— If you're ill, make an appointment with a reputable naturopathic doctor or healer to see what she has to say. Does she know others who have healed themselves from the same illness? Be open to trying something new.

3. *Fire:* Vocation

As you look at your Life Garden plan, what seeds have you planted for your vocation that you want to see grow—a new job, your life's work or calling, a purpose? What can you do to tap into the power of your passion and grow in this area? How does it make you feel to have work that you love?

— If you're overworked in a salaried position, cut back to just 40 hours for one week and see what happens.

— Make up business cards or a website with your dream job, and then tell people that's what you do. How do others react to your dream job versus what you do today? How does it feel?

4. *Air:* Relationships

As you look at your Life Garden plan, what seeds have you planted for relationships that you want to see grow—family, significant other, friends? What can you do to harness the power of the air and bring the right new relationships into your life? How does it feel to be spending time with people who bring you energy and joy and share your love of life?

— If you're missing sensuality in your life, start wearing sexy underwear (guys, this means you, too) and see how that changes how you feel and act throughout the day. No one will know you're wearing it, but you'll feel different—and people will react to you differently as well.

— If you're having a difficult time with someone at work, don't confront him and try to control how he feels or force him to do something your way. Instead, focus on the relationship you want during your daily meditation, and then treat that person the way you'd like to be treated. Rather than being upset with him, you'll now have a deeper sense of compassion. See how this internal shift changes the relationship at work without the need to do anything confrontational.

5. *Spirit:* **Creative Expression**

As you look at your Life Garden plan, what seeds have you planted for creative expression that you want to see grow—hobbies, talents, possibilities? What can you do to tap into the spirit and power of the Universe and express yourself creatively in the world? How does it feel to be truly articulating the essence of you?

— Try something new with your appearance, such as a different hairstyle. Or experiment with outrageous apparel you normally wouldn't wear—a sexy or sophisticated outfit, a hat, a new sport coat, or spiked heels. How does it make you feel? How are people reacting to you, and how does *that* make you feel?

— Take a class in something you love to do—storytelling, dancing, cooking, playing the piano, pottery, biking, or what have you. Do it this week and see how it makes you feel.

Now that you have a list of ideas, dare to go out and do some of these activities over the next few days or weeks, and then pay attention to what happens. Ask yourself how you feel in each of these scenarios. How do other people react—and how do you react to their reactions? Do you still hold the same beliefs? Did you learn anything about yourself? If so, what was it? Did you decide to change anything in your garden?

This exercise is a lot of fun because it helps you experience the world in a whole new way. You may think you're not a "hat person," for instance . . . until you find that when you put on a beautiful chapeau and walk the streets of your city, everyone looks at you differently and your day is completely changed.

It's our preconceptions and preprogrammed beliefs about life that have gone unquestioned that prevent us from expressing and experiencing what's true for us. When we take action—actually experience a change—it encourages us to grow.

Business Is Personal

As I started to connect with what was really important to me and how I wanted to declare my freedom, I made some changes in the way I did things at work. I was no longer afraid to be myself, nor did I feel compelled to dress or act in a certain way because I was in a business situation.

Many people say "business is business," but I could never understand how people can be one way at work and another way with their family and friends. The boundaries especially blur for us entrepreneurs, because we're working when we go to the mall, hire a plumber, or go to the dentist, as well as when we work with a printer or an advertising agency. All these dealings involve people, and business that involves people is always personal.

When I started my own company, I began to wear clothes that were comfortable for me, since I didn't feel as if I needed to wear a suit to show my competence. I found that wearing casual clothes to meet new clients set a relaxed and warm tone for our relationship right from the very beginning, and we were both free to be more comfortable while working together.

Although countless individuals wear casual clothes to work, there are still many companies and people who feel that the "proper" attire for a professional businessperson is either a suit and tie (for a man) or a skirt and blazer (for a woman). This brings to mind one of my older clients, who knew me in my suit-and-stockings days. Although she'd always been very friendly to me, that stopped when I changed my formal approach. She made it very difficult for me to be in meetings I really needed to attend, often not inviting me to them at all, and pretty much stopped communicating with me altogether. Another colleague noticed this shift in demeanor and made sure I knew about any pertinent meetings, but it was really awkward for everyone involved.

I later found out that this woman ran her own department through fear. She thrived on rules and regulations, and it was her way or the highway. When I was once five minutes late for a meeting and was wearing jeans, that's when she decided to stop talking to me.

In her mind, I was unprofessional. End of story. But what she didn't know was that the man who had hired me, one of her peers, was aware that I'd be late for the meeting and had approved my wearing jeans to their office.

I learned here that when we start making changes to bring our Life Gardens into better alignment with what we envision for ourselves, not everyone is going to respond in a positive way. But instead of going against my truth and changing to please this woman, I decided to focus on my heart and align with what was right for me.

In my Life Garden, I saw myself working harmoniously with all of my co-workers in my casual clothes. I also saw myself acting in a professional manner and working toward positive outcomes for everyone involved. I focused on rooting in my own beliefs, I nourished myself when I was going to come in contact with this woman, and I worked on demonstrating harmonious solutions whenever possible.

As I cleaned up my field internally—through my nourishment, meditation, and actions in other areas of my life—I started to see shifts in the older woman. I never had to confront her or write a long and confrontational e-mail . . . in fact, I didn't have to do anything. I just sent loving and healing energy to her and changed my view of the situation. I had compassion for this woman, because I knew that she must be going through something more difficult than I could see and was just trying to exert some power and control in her life.

It didn't happen overnight, but after a while she started to open up to me again. If I had given in and either conformed to this one person's idea of professionalism or apologized for something I didn't feel was wrong, then I would have come out of my alignment with self and hindered my own positive growth.

It's important to insist on what we know is true, and to always stick to our guns. I call this our "Flower Power." We might not be able to change other people, but we *are* able to control our thoughts, beliefs, and responses. I did the work in my own Garden first and saw the changes—the beautiful blooms—manifest in my external world. I shifted how I viewed the situation and did the work inside myself, relying on the power of my heart.

In the end, I was absolutely amazed by how good I felt. My client and I were able to come to a resolution without confrontation or power plays. And best of all, we both grew through the experience:

I grew in my confidence, courage, and connection to my heart; and the woman grew by learning to accept people for who they are instead of trying so hard to control everyone around her through fear. She loosened her grip and saw that my intentions were good and pure, and that I could still be professional and smart even though I wasn't wearing a suit. Everyone involved had grown through change.

Jan Wikman's Story

For me, business is personal. I have always been able to make very close friendships through my work colleagues, create incredible strategies, and be there for personal life events as well. I've found that when you add another, spiritual, dimension to the work equation, then work is definitely more than just that. This is how it is with my friend and colleague Jan Wikman.

Jan and I were destined to meet—our paths have crossed several times throughout our careers, but it was just recently that we really connected. We were working on a project together, and our relationship could have remained purely professional as we went through tasks, met our objectives, and exchanged cordial e-mails. Yet when we had a moment to talk privately, I felt I needed to tell her about the new direction my career had taken.

Immediately, the conversation changed, and Jan said, "I've got to tell you a story." And I knew I had to share that story with others. . . .

Jan has spent most of her career as an activator, driving change within organizations as well as modifying consumer behavior. She's always been a big player in the consumer-loyalty and promotion fields, working with companies such as Best Buy, Microsoft, AT&T, T-Mobile, General Mills, and Target. She then took a job as the vice president of sales and operations for Young America Corporation, the largest consumer-promotion company in the United States. Here, she was responsible for driving and managing more than 350 million consumer interactions annually on behalf of her clients. She was busy and successful, but this wasn't enough for Jan. She wanted more meaning and purpose in her job so that she could make a difference in the world.

In addition to taking classes and buffing up her professional skills, Jan had always done her own personal and spiritual work. She understood that we're all responsible for creating our own Life Gardens and had always trusted in her ability to co-create her life with the assistance of the Universal Power. Jan knew that if we are willing to live our lives with integrity and are aware of how and where we focus our energy, then anything is possible, personally and professionally. So she meditated daily, trusted her intuition, and maintained an unwavering faith that she would be taken care of as long as she remained true to her connection.

Since Jan didn't feel that she was able to remain true to herself in her job at Young America, she planted her personal Seeds of Freedom in her Life Garden and waited to see what happened. As if by magic, she was offered a promotion at her current job— and then she got a phone call from another company, asking her to lead up a new division that would be focused on helping consumers make more nutritious food choices.

Jan evaluated both opportunities and decided to go with her gut. Although BI Worldwide was one of the leading loyalty marketing companies in the world, and they were offering her a wonderful position, it was still a risk. Yet she wanted to make a difference, and this job felt right to her. Before long, the new division she'd been asked to run, called EcoBonus, was thriving. Jan is now vice president of sales and operations for EcoBonus, which brings together a coalition of leading manufacturers, retailers, and service providers who want to reach and reward consumers interested in learning about and making more sustainable choices.

The concept of coalition is very powerful and has been a great model for programs such as Box Tops for Education, which Jan helped launch with General Mills. And she's now able to integrate her personal convictions in doing the right thing and collaborating to create a new way of doing business with consumers, other companies, the earth, and the energy around us. It's a win-win for everyone, especially for Jan.

She wants to "move the middle" by generating significant consumer action. Her vision for EcoBonus is to create a movement that empowers individuals to make better choices for their lives, their families, and perhaps the world by leveraging the power of business. She *knows* that she is in the right job for her and will be able to give consumers more choices, freedom, and buying power by giving this population a voice.

I think Jan is on to something. She's thriving in all areas of her Life Garden and is able to live her life in integrity at home and at work. The business relationship she and I have hasn't been the same, however. It's not just business now—it's personal, spiritual, collaborative, and fun. Our relationship is "more than," and we sure like it that way.

You Grow, Girl!

As I've mentioned before, with pain and suffering comes growth. I've found that every event in life has a purpose and every struggle brings a lesson. I see my own failures as personal expansion leading me to inner growth and spiritual awakening, and I understand how these failures are inextricably linked together to help me unearth my life purpose. It's those difficult and humbling experiences that led me to be the person I am today, and I fully embrace that person.

Often people will ask me if I regret staying in a demanding job for so long, being in a relationship that ended in betrayal, or not getting married and having children. Although I might make some different choices now, I certainly don't regret any of my decisions. These some-times uncomfortable and agonizing situations were the catalysts for my growth. And because I know this pain intimately, I'm able to talk about it openly with knowledge and understanding. It also helps me know when I'm feeling good—that is, when I've hit the high points. Contrast in life helps all of us grow.

There are no mistakes in life—only lessons or opportunities to evolve and learn more. Pain and struggle have been great teachers because they forced me to seek out new solutions, discover my own truths, break down false assumptions, and expand my thinking. Each situation led me to seek higher ground, dig deeper into my soul, and unearth the most vulnerable and sensitive parts of myself. And that's where the good stuff is.

Not long ago, I used to beat myself up when I took what I per-ceived to be a misstep. Now, I celebrate all the opportunities I get to learn and don't see the difficult times, the endings, or the annoying little flare-ups in life as things that are bad or that should be avoided. I know that I'll benefit from life experience, so now I just tell myself, "You grow, girl!" in the midst of difficulties. Everything I go through helps me identify what I need to work on so that I can plant a new life of freedom.

Just as in a garden, growth is a never-ending process of life, death, and rebirth. There is no beginning and no end. We're never going to be where we want to be. We'll always want more; we'll always want to experience new things; and we'll always want to reach for bigger, better, or different dreams. That's just how we're wired. So if we can get comfortable being in the space between where we are and where we want to be, then we will be living in the moment and constantly striving for more. *We'll be growing.*

We're always creating, refining, and expanding our Life Garden plan, so if we want to continue to experience life to the fullest and live out our dreams, then it's our decision to choose growth. If we aren't growing, then we're dying; and if we're dying, we're not free.

Now that we've rooted in ourselves and opened our heart, we're going to learn about the power of trusting our intuition to help grow a Life Garden that matters. The next seed we're going to plant is that of connection.

Digging Deeper: Follow Your Heart

To dig deeper and help your Life Garden grow and flourish, you can:

1. Read *The Biology of Belief* by Dr. Bruce Lipton. In this book, the author uses simple language to explain groundbreaking work in new biology, which explains the power of the connection between our mind and body and the biological processes. He's discovered that our minds and hearts control our biology, not the genes and DNA that we've been taught to believe. If you're open to challenging your beliefs and learning about the power of your thoughts and emotions, then this will be a life-changing book for you. It certainly was for me.

2. Think with your heart. Whatever you want to grow in your Life Garden, start to grow it in your heart first. And when you think about something, engage your heart, too. As you start to "think" with your heart, you'll be digging deeper into your desires, tapping into the power of your heart, and opening yourself up so that more things will be able to come into your Life Garden.

3. Check out the Institute of HeartMath (at www.heart math.org). This is an internationally recognized nonprofit research-and-education organization, which is focused on helping people build resilience for happy and healthy lives by reducing stress and regulating emotions through heart coherence. HeartMath offers training to help people tune in to the intelligence of their hearts at work, home, school, and play. The research available through this organization is simply fascinating.

◎ ◎ ◎

CHAPTER SIX

CONNECTION

"All human beings are interconnected,
one with all other elements in creation."

— HENRY REED

Life is made up of a series of connections: to self, to other people, and to all things in the Universe. Everything is connected to everything. If we can see past the flat surfaces and look into the multidimensionality—the depth, breadth, and reach—of each connection, we'd be overwhelmed by the impact we have on the world. As we change, the world will change . . . but the world can change us, too.

Right now, the earth is going through a massive social, environmental, and astrological upheaval; there is a systematic breaking down of the old to make way for the new. And all of these planetary shifts are directly affecting our personal lives: think of the major natural disasters in Haiti and Japan, the financial meltdown on Wall Street, and the political uprisings across the globe.

So much change is opening our hearts, enabling us to connect with our authentic selves—the parts of us that are natural, divine, and unburdened by the rules of our society. We're now moving from a place of structure, conformity, and facts to one of fluidity, individuality, and intuition. As we bring awareness to the fleeting nature of life, and understand that all things are temporary, we're able to communicate with everything. Through a connection with ourselves, we can then connect with other human beings, as well as spiritual realms. We can connect to true joy and freedom.

Once we welcome the invisible realm of spirit, synchronicity, and miracles into our lives, we start to experience the world in a very different manner. Everything becomes easier, and magic starts to happen. Yet since many factors are involved on our spiritual journey of meaning, we need to be realistic about what we can expect and have faith that we're on the right path. It took us a long time to become who we are, and our habits cannot be changed overnight.

Having said that, when we open up to this source energy, then we start to receive nourishment that most individuals are not getting in their fast-paced, busy lives. As we cultivate our connection, our roots grow deeper and deeper, allowing us to tap into the power of the Universe. We're able to soak up this nourishment and then use the added energy to create beautiful things in our Life Gardens and in the world around us.

It's hard to imagine at first, but once we are aligned with the essence of who we are and are aware of the connection we have to our energy source, then we're inviting magic to come into our orbit. Life becomes easy, magnificent, and expansive. Our only responsibility is to tend to our own growth and create from our hearts.

At work, we're often ruled by facts and figures. The business world is full of justification and projections based on the statistics of past history, blended with our expectations and best guesses. We want to see something, justify it, and then accurately predict its future. We have to play by the rules, procedures, guidelines, and protocol. We overlook the natural aspects of our environment—the things that cost nothing and can easily lead to greater success, innovation, and unlimited possibilities.

Many successful executives use intuition to help them professionally. They may be reluctant to discuss it with their peers, but it definitely gives them a competitive advantage over those business-people who aren't connected to their inner knowing.

Lisa Arie's Story

At some point in life, everyone is presented with a choice to either continue on the path of the known or to step off into the unknown. One way seems familiar, safe, and secure; while the other offers that which is unfamiliar, messy, and uncertain. My friend Lisa Arie faced such a choice when she decided to follow her heart and move from the certainty and familiarity of New York to the hinterlands of southwest Colorado.

From the outside, it looked like Lisa had it all. She was beautiful, fit, socially active, and the owner of a multimillion-dollar boutique creative-resource company in New York City. But on the inside, she felt disconnected from the success she was creating around her. She felt lost and alone, as if her life was passing her by. Her existence seemed meaningless, beyond the basics of creating an income to support and enhance her days.

Lisa had dutifully followed the path laid out before her as a little girl—get a job, get married, and live happily ever after. Yet although she seemed to have it all, she wasn't happy and knew something was missing. Then one day she realized the path she was on wasn't her own, and the key that was missing was her.

Productivity and results had always brought rewards to Lisa. Somewhere along the line, however, the rewards stopped being fulfilling, and a vast emptiness filled their place. She knew there had to be more to life, but she didn't know where to find it. This "missing piece" didn't seem to be something that could be bought in a store or found in another one of her entrepreneurial creations.

What this woman learned as she let go and stepped into the unfamiliar was that she was seeking a relationship with herself. She wanted a genuine, unconditional connection and understanding of who she really was, without all the hype and noise. This direction wasn't something that came from her mind—it came from her heart. It wasn't logical, but it felt right. She followed the feeling.

Lisa found what was missing when she inadvertently and unexpectedly connected with horses. She'd ridden them as a little girl, but it was nothing more than one of those things she did as she was growing up, like ice skating or finger painting. Now, horses opened her up to parts of herself she'd shut down long ago, and in ways she never dreamed possible. She got dirty mucking stalls and tending to the creatures in the rain and sleet, but she was the happiest she'd ever been. The horses showed her how to open her heart and tune in to all of her senses. It didn't happen overnight, but she kept moving forward on her true path, step-by-step, as she built trust and love within herself. She was then able to take that love and trust and connect with people in a way she hadn't known was possible.

As my friend continued on this path, her internal world expanded, which seemed to magically and mysteriously expand her external world exponentially. She felt a sense of inner security; and a new understanding of love, courage, and vitality grew from that. As she embraced this newfound sense of security fully, it afforded her the opportunity to pursue a more authentic life for herself. Consequently, she moved to Colorado to commit to a life with her horses.

Lisa continues to discover that, as she embraces her calling, her life becomes enriched in every arena. For example, she met and married a man who shares her love and her life. And she's taken what she's learned from her dear horses and created an experiential-learning facility on 160 private acres of rich land. Vista Caballo Innovation Ranch helps others connect to their natural instincts as they begin their own modern-day rite of passage from the comfortable and familiar into the new and unexpected.

Lisa feels that she is definitely on the right path now, and there's no longer anything missing. To me, she's living proof that you can have it all if you follow your heart, do the work, and trust your inner voice. As she says, "Listening to that voice is the start of your transformation. Trusting is the key to freedom."

When we follow our hearts and trust our intuition, we quickly discover what is possible and right for us. We can use our intuition to make big life decisions, such as whom to marry or what job to take; along with smaller decisions, such as whether to have coffee or tea, or go to yoga class or for a run. When we listen to our inner knowing and act on inspired action, then we don't have to "make things happen"; we don't have to expend any effort on going through the motions or continue to stay in a painful situation. There is no secret formula for accessing our intuition—nor do we have to buy, do, or have anything first. It's simple, and it's free.

Since I've been connected to the flow of the Universe, I always manage to get seated next to the right person on airplanes, make the right phone call at the right time, or show up at just the right networking event when the people I'm destined to meet will be present. I don't try to make anything happen anymore; rather, I just listen to what I need to do for the next step.

Connecting to your own intuition will save you time and effort because you'll know that you're always where you're supposed to be. Logic doesn't apply all the time; listening to your gut instinct can be far more helpful for you. Not only will your intuition help you cultivate your inner Garden and gain power over your life, but it can also help you have more satisfying relationships and successful outcomes, both personally and professionally.

When you connect to the essence of who you are, a new way of living emerges. Your job is less mundane. Your existence has more meaning and purpose. You see yourself as part of something bigger, and can even see the specific role you play. The Universe starts to work in your favor, and beneficial allies and circumstances show up seemingly from out of nowhere.

Magic in your Life Garden unlocks your spirit easily, as it offers secrets that are whispered in the rustle of the leaves, the chirp of the birds, or the swaying of the trees. As you change how you communicate, you transform your connections and ultimately your life—your relationships, your work, your health, and your creativity.

Trusting Your Inner Voice

Don't go in the water! I kept hearing a loud voice repeating these words over and over in my head as I walked through an Indian meditation garden. This was my second trip to India, and this time it was a spiritual journey. I'd come a very long way to visit this particular ashram and wanted to experience the healing benefits of the Theerthakund, a subterranean pool with a solidified mercury lingam in the water. It was supposed to have amazing healing benefits and positive spiritual energy.

It's a tradition in India to wet the entire body prior to entering a temple to help make the body more receptive to the energy—and I needed all the good energy I could get! All I could think about was that I'd traveled to the other side of the globe to experience bathing in these sacred waters, only to have a voice in my head scream that I shouldn't do it.

The friends I was traveling with, Binoti and Nirmala, had already broached the possibility of contracting a disease or some sort of infection if we stepped into these waters. Here we were, in a country where we had to close our eyes and mouths when we showered, use bottled water to brush our teeth, and make sure we didn't get ice in any of our drinks or eat vegetables that hadn't been cooked or peeled, for fear of getting dysentery or some other kind of unmentionable ailment. India is not an easy country to travel in, and we had to be cautious about everything we did every minute of the day. Yet my friends didn't have any hesitation about going into the pool before we entered the temple.

We were all exhausted from traveling, and I wasn't sure if the voice in my head was my instinct assisting me or my fear of getting some kind of disease popping to the surface. Either way, I was trying so hard to trust my intuition to make decisions instead of using my comfortable, left-brained, logical approach. I hemmed and hawed, and then I finally decided to ignore the voice in my head and the knot in my stomach and join Binoti and Nirmala in the pool. When in Rome (or India, in this case), right?

We'd come all this way to connect to the energy of this one ashram, and I really wanted it to happen. My can-do attitude and my ego kicked in, and I was going to push through my fear so that I could say I'd done so. I'd also be able to find out what going in this infused water would do to me—I wanted instant manifestation. I thought that the more energy or assistance I could harness, the better. So I totally disregarded my inner voice and decided to go in the water.

What I'd overlooked was that I'd created a Life Garden plan that was moving me away from the "Just do it" mentality. In the process, I had invited the seed of connection into my Garden and was slowly learning to distinguish between my intuition and my logical mind. I was discovering that when I connected to my inner knowledge and the spiritual part of myself, I didn't have to carry the burden of every decision or outcome. I was learning to trust that nature, the Universe, or the people in my life would assist in a natural unfolding, which would result in a positive outcome for everyone involved. I was getting to the point that "just doing it" and pushing through fear or hesitation wasn't working for me anymore. Nevertheless, I'd forgotten about the seed of connection here at the ashram because it was still so small that it wasn't visible in my Garden.

I wanted to honor what was right for me—I'd asked to hear my inner voice, and even though I should have trusted it, I didn't. So Binoti, Nirmala, and I headed down to the pool on this damp and rainy night. I pulled on a saffron-colored sari, tied it with a rope, and headed off to the pool to submerge myself in the sacred waters. I was still nervous, my stomach was clenched, and I was replaying my decision over and over in my head. But I was determined to push through the fear.

As soon as my friends and I walked up to the entrance, we saw a sign that said MEN. We had somehow confused our schedule and missed the last time that women could enter the pool. *Really?* This felt like a cosmic joke. Was the Universe trying to teach me something? I just laughed as I realized that spirit really was trying to assist me. I wasn't supposed to go in that water.

At that moment, I remembered a quote from Ralph Waldo Emerson: "Trust the instinct to the end, though you can render no reason." I didn't know the reason why I wasn't supposed to go in the water, but I did learn a lesson about trusting my instinct and intuition. I didn't need to figure anything out, analyze the situation, or listen to other people's opinions. The answer was blaring in my head.

I realized that although I'd known what was right for me, I hadn't wanted to miss out on anything, so I'd blatantly ignored my inner knowing and hadn't trusted the guidance that had been given to me through connection. But because I'd begun to connect to the Universe, the Universe had reached out and stopped me. Right then, I learned that I could have faith in the Universe to take care of me, even when I thought that I knew better.

We need to remember that when we're rooted in ourselves and connected to our intuition, there is always spiritual assistance looking out for us. It may not appear as we envisioned it, and it's nothing we can plan. Many times we dismiss it or are too wrapped up in trying to figure out the solution to even hear the message from spirit, or we don't trust the message if we do hear it. This, of course, is what happened to me. I heard a very clear message and ignored it—and the alignment of events prevented me from going in the water anyway. Who knows what would have happened if I'd gone in?

Ultimately, the trip to the ashram turned out to be well worth the journey. Binoti, Nirmala, and I could feel the sacredness of this place the moment the taxi driver dropped us at the front gate. We enjoyed several meditations, contemplation in the garden, and a special full-moon ceremony while we were there. The energy there not only taught me a vivid lesson in trusting my intuition, but it catapulted my spiritual journey into a new dimension as well.

Even though I never went in the sacred pool, I did experience something incredible, life changing, mind-blowing, and surreal at the ashram. It's always difficult to explain these types of experiences as they're so subjective, personal, and multidimensional—but during one of the meditations, I felt such a physical, mental, and spiritual connection that energy currents were rushing through my entire body. I felt totally and completely at one with the Universe and was interconnected with all things. I had no end and no beginning. My spirit extended out past the edges of my physical body toward the whole world, and everything was alive and full of possibility. I was love itself.

This was one of those things that is often called "indescribable" . . . and it really was. It's like trying to tell someone how raspberries taste or what holding your baby for the first time feels like. You can't really describe it; you have to experience it for yourself to know its effect on you.

As I hope my story has illustrated, the most critical attribute any of us can have when planting our Life Gardens is the connection to our internal guidance system, which comes from the power of our hearts. As our roots continue to grow, they're able to provide our hearts with the nourishment or courage they require to open and expand. And this growth gives us access to our hearts' desires, our connection to nature, and our intuition.

We all have the answers inside of us—and if we want to keep moving toward freedom, we need to open our hearts, listen, and trust our inner guidance. When we start to see the synchronicities and meaningful coincidences in our lives, then we know we're on the right path.

Connect to Your Intuition

As your Life Garden grows and expands toward your vision, you're going to be called to explore new terrain, such as the wilderness of your intuition. This will probably be unfamiliar territory, but what you'll discover is a new way of being, a fresh way of experiencing your life, and a wonderful way to discover your own truths.

Are you open to the unknowns of business, or do you have to stick to "the plan"? Are you willing to alter that plan—or even drop it completely—if something unexpected comes along that could bring you success beyond your wildest dreams? Connecting to your intuition means that you've got to be open to the unexpected. It could be defined as "perceiving or knowing something without conscious reasoning." In other words, it's when you have a strong feeling that something's going to happen, without anything logical to back up that feeling.

When you've tapped into your intuition, you leave the house at exactly the right time; show up early for a meeting, which happens to be when your client is there and wants to brainstorm; or instinctively switch lanes on the highway to miss something blocking the road. Intuition is strongly related to the heart center. So when you accept that your heart has information that isn't accessed by your brain—and that you can train yourself to tap into your sixth sense, gut feelings, or hunches—then you're able to accept your place in the world and relate to your environment.

Intuition is our internal compass or guiding force in life, which leads us to our highest potential. When we're using that internal compass, then we understand what our Life Gardens need, just like a mother's intuition tells her why her child is crying. We just know. Our Gardens are our personal life plans; since we're the only ones who clearly understand what we want to achieve, we don't need to talk about it too much or overanalyze what needs to be done next. We can sense what we need to do to stay on our right path: our path of freedom.

We do this by paying attention to our environment and trusting that everything is in harmony, even when it feels as if we're in the midst of chaos. If we listen with our hearts and open up to the possibilities in the world around us, then we're able to release control of the outcome, surrender to nature's wisdom, and develop the inner power that comes from connecting to our intuition.

Now that your personal Life Garden is starting to grow, what is it saying to you? Did you plant the right seeds? Do you have too much or too little of something? How do you feel? Are you struggling? Thriving? As the gardener of your life, you must trust that your Garden is going to flourish, and stay open to the magic that wants to assist you in your creation. Try to resist the urge to control every single aspect of your Garden—this type of micromanaging prevents the magic that would make things much easier. If you can get quiet and open your heart, then you can get a glimpse of your interconnection with the world around you. It's when you have an open heart that you can trust, and allow nature's mystery to unfold.

Exercise: Develop Your Intuition

If you want to get in touch with your intuition, the first thing you need to do is slow down and just allow yourself to be. Close your eyes; take some deep breaths; and then ask yourself some questions, being sure to listen to the answers that pop into your mind. Don't just pay attention to your thoughts; also note the images, feelings, and other physical sensations you experience. By learning to connect with your intuition, you'll be able to connect with the invisible information present in the Universe—the power that created all things in our world.

Instead of doing things for the sake of doing them, listen for inspired action. Are you inspired to go to the store now? If so, then there's bound to be something more waiting for you as you do that task.

An activity-centered life is based upon doing activities because we're supposed to do them, they need to be done, or we want to make something happen. Inspired action is about taking the time to slow down and listen to ourselves so that we can hear what we need to do next on our journeys. It comes from a place of trust, belief, and allowing, so that the Universe can conspire in our favor.

As you start to connect to your intuition, new information will come to mind. Act on it. It may be a beautiful day outside, yet you get the feeling to go back in the house and grab your umbrella. Don't think about it—just act on your intuition. Intuition is like a muscle and you need to flex it, listen to it, and act on the information you receive. You'll start to see synchronicities occur in your life, events will flow to you easily, and doors will open that may have been closed before.

Keep paying attention to the information you receive and ask yourself the following:

- What am I ready to act on now?
- Which choice brings me the most vitality?
- How do I feel about my choice?

As you build your awareness of the power and accuracy of your intuition, keep track in your journal of how many of your hunches actually come through for you. Record the images that come to your mind when you're dreaming, or how you're feeling when you do activities that you enjoy.

You can also set aside a time once a day to check in and write down any observations, thoughts, feelings, or synchronicities. For example, maybe you were thinking of someone, and at that very moment, the person called you. Or you stopped off at a coffee shop and, completely by chance, ran into a friend you'd been meaning to reconnect with. Perhaps something told you not to hit SEND on that angry e-mail you wrote at work—and by the end of the day, you were glad you hadn't, because the situation had entirely resolved itself in your favor.

> The most important thing is to be patient and listen. Answers don't always come right away, but they *will* come. When you open the door to a new dimension in your life, be gentle with yourself and allow things to unfold naturally.

As I began to connect to my intuition, I thought about water all the time. There was water everywhere in my thoughts, dreams, and visions. Every fiber in my being wanted to be near the smell of the ocean instead of in a landlocked city full of smog. Fortunately, I already had a small condo at the beach that used to be a rental property. More and more, I contemplated using it for myself.

As I spent more time in my Life Garden exploring, focusing, rooting, nourishing, and growing, I started to change. When I first planned my Garden, it was mainly about security. I was focused on creating a stable life with a house, a husband, children, a career, and financial security. These things were so important to me because they represented someone who was solid, lovable, and had purpose. However, as I challenged my beliefs, test-drove what I thought I wanted, and really connected to my innermost desires, my Life Garden vision began to transform.

I found that I preferred to spend time at my little condo in Hilton Head Island, South Carolina, than in my big house in Atlanta. I preferred to meditate rather than mingle, cook at home rather than go out, get my hands dirty in the garden rather than get a manicure at the spa, and create rather than conform. I concluded that it was time to put my house in Atlanta up for sale and spend more time in Hilton Head, enjoying solitude, walks on the beach, and time on the tennis court.

I drove back and forth between Atlanta and Hilton Head every other week, bringing some of my belongings with me each time so that I could slowly move things where I wanted them to be. It was about a five-hour drive each way, but I was happy doing it because it was getting me closer to the life I wanted to live. My entire family lived in Hilton Head, so I relished the thought that I'd have more time with my parents, sister, and twin nephews.

On one such trip, I was about an hour into the drive when I had a strong feeling that I'd get a flat tire. I pulled over and checked all four tires, but I didn't see anything wrong. It was late in the day, and I didn't have time to figure out where to go to have a mechanic check everything thoroughly. So I took a deep breath, connected to my intuition, and asked my higher self if I'd be okay if I continued on my journey. I had a strong sense that if I did get a flat tire, help would arrive promptly, and the entire situation would resolve itself easily and quickly.

About 30 minutes later, I was talking to my mother on the phone when I heard a big pop and started to lose control of the car. I was able to pull off the road safely to see that I did indeed have a flat tire. Before I could even dial the number for AAA to get some assistance, a car pulled over, and a man got out asking if he could help me change the tire. In less than ten minutes, he'd put the spare on, and I was on my way.

This man and I had exchanged business cards, so the next morning, I sent him an e-mail to thank him. I let him know that I'd arrived at my destination safely and told him that he was my "guardian angel." Here was his reply:

> *Heather, I am so glad you made it home safely! I wondered if you made it. You are very welcome. I was actually planning on heading home earlier that day, but for some reason I stayed in Atlanta a little longer. Now I know that God wanted me to change your tire. The Holy Spirit moves us quite often, we just have to pay attention. God bless you.*

When we're connected to our intuition, to our higher selves, or to God, then we are *always* protected. I had a strong knowing that everything would be okay and saved myself hours of time trying to find a service station and waiting to have them check out my tires. I got the okay to keep driving. And the man who stopped to help me was also connected—this seemed to be the reason he'd stayed in Atlanta longer than he'd planned.

By paying attention to messages like these, we can allow synchronicity to give us a magical helping hand.

Connect to Empathy

When we plant a tomato plant in our yard, we don't get mad at it if it fails to grow the way we'd hoped or blame it for not being good enough. Instead, we look at the environment for reasons why that tomato plant isn't growing well, and try to adjust our own care of the plant so that it can flourish. We check the temperature and amount of sunlight, we feel the dirt to see if it needs more or less water, we look for bugs, and we decide if the plant needs fertilizer. We look at all the conditions and then listen to the tomato plant and our intuition to determine what it needs.

Unfortunately, we often aren't as kind in our personal relationships. We get upset when people don't live up to our expectations, perform the way we want them to, or grow fast enough. But if we would take the time to observe *all* the factors in others' lives instead of blaming them or arguing with them, maybe we'd be more likely to understand where they're coming from. If we'd just connect to empathy, we might be able to intuitively hear what they need in order to improve their growth.

When it feels as if other people are being unrealistic, attacking you, or making you suffer, consider that maybe they're behaving this way because they're suffering inside and projecting their fear onto you. Develop empathy for the pain they're struggling with—and instead of going to battle to defend yourself, shift your energy from within. Tap into the love you have for yourself, the confidence you feel in your truth, and the compassion you feel for other human beings. Replace self-doubt with self-love, and you'll soon be amazed by how the dynamic improves between you and those who are taking issue with you. Remember, when you shift your internal world, the external world shifts as well.

Relationships with others will help guide you to your own authentic place. And whenever you bump up against any obstacle—be it a person, thing, or incident—it aids you in your Life Garden. As you bring awareness to these connections, then no matter what's happening, you can trust that your Garden is growing exactly as it's supposed to. You're learning how to tap into the natural cycles of life, as well as into your own internal guidance system, which will help you navigate your way to the Garden you desire.

If you develop a sense of empathy with others, then your mind opens up and you can see the world as a place of interconnectedness and kindness. If you only think of yourself, then you'll stay narrow-minded and small. But the secret here is that you nourish yourself first so that you can then love others unconditionally. The more you connect to yourself, the more you can connect to others and have the strength and courage to forgive, be openhearted, and understand where they're coming from. You can feel for them, and bring about harmony and healing.

Exercise: **What's Really Going On?**

This quick exercise always helps my clients figure out what's really going on beneath the surface of a potential conflict. Try it yourself, writing down your responses in your journal:

Situation: You don't understand why someone is acting in a certain way. Perhaps you feel singled out, attacked, left out, victimized, or controlled. The action this person has taken doesn't make sense, and you'd like to handle the situation in a different manner.

— Write down the name of the person.

— Describe the problem.

— Why does this bother you?

— What is he or she projecting—blame, fear, anger, insecurity, control?

— Is there potentially another reason why this individual could be projecting this emotion toward you?

— Close your eyes. Think about the person from a place of compassion, and ask your intuition what is going on with him or her. Listen, and write down what you hear.

— Close your eyes. Think about how you'd like the relationship to be, and ask your intuition what you can do to defuse the situation. Listen, and write down what you hear.

When we truly connect with other people, our personal relations can help us learn, connect in a shared purpose, and evoke the collective intelligence of the Universe to expand and flourish in our common goals. It's important that we relate to each other as fellow human beings, though—when we treat others the way we want to be treated, then we can see ourselves in them and remember that we're all equal. Whatever we give, we get in return, so it's important to sincerely treat all of those who come into our Life Gardens the same. We all matter. We can change lives when we treat people with respect, regardless of their title, authority, or appearance.

When you connect to humanity, you will be more loving, compassionate, and altruistic. Altruism is a basic human characteristic, and when it becomes part of your life, you reap more health benefits than you could imagine. Being of service can be done in so many ways, and you can make a difference in a way that feels right to you. Find your gift and then share it. It might be your smile, your cooking, or your kind words at work. You can make the world a better place just by doing your part in society—by being compassionate and present, and by caring for other people and the planet. Your energy and intention will truly shine through and make an impact.

Everything we do in our Life Gardens—what we grow, how we express ourselves, and how involved we are in our communities— matters. Therefore, our connection to empathy not only strengthens our own Gardens, but it also helps other people in the world through the simple act of sharing. We share information, abundance, time, experiences, and love. A community gives us strength and a system to support one another. This is the biggest shift that we need to make in today's society.

Connecting isn't always easy, but connecting deeply with others means that our hearts are opening, and we're being courageous and vulnerable. And although this can be scary, our connections help us learn and join us with something greater in the world.

Connect to All Life in the Universe

Our beautiful, bountiful, life-giving planet is home to many diverse communities, and most ancient traditions believe that it is alive and connected to everything else. Religious texts use stories involving the earth's wind, water, deserts, mountains, animals, and seasons to help us understand the divine nature of human life. Many believe that when we hurt our planet, we're hurting our own consciousness and our very existence; we cannot survive, let alone flourish, without Mother Earth's well-being and wholeness.

Gregg Braden, a former computer geologist, has studied indigenous cultures all over the world to uncover the Universe's timeless secrets. Gregg believes that we're all connected to the earth, spiritual forces, and creation; and he now presents these findings in his books and speeches. In an interview published in the Webzine *The Spirit of Ma'at* (**www.spiritofmaat.com/archive/jul3/braden.htm**), he shared the following:

> Almost universally, ancient texts and traditions say to us, in the language of their time, that we are part of all that we see, that we are related through a Force to the events of our world, to one another, to the processes within our bodies and the Cosmos and beyond. In our most sacred traditions, this Force is described as all-powerful, something that permeates all of Creation. It's not "out there" somewhere. It is a part of ourselves as well as a part of all that we perceive.

All life is interconnected and interdependent on this sacred planet, and we need to protect Earth's ecological diversity, beauty, and health. It's the diversity that gives us our freedom and balance. Mother Earth has rhythms, seasons, and systems that support and guide us; without her, there are no gardens.

When we garden, we commune with nature, and we appreciate the way everything on our planet is interconnected with everything else. When we approach our lives with the same care and attention as a gardener tends to his or her plot, then we're strengthening our connection to the earth. We pay more attention to our surroundings and the meaning behind everyday occurrences. We're more prepared for any season or situation, as well as being open to the synchronicity in life.

As our roots grow, we connect to the world of spirit and are able to form deeper connections with the world around us. When we're focused on something and open to its arrival in our lives, then it starts to appear as if by magic. We just need to get out of the way and receive it. That's when we shift from a mere existence to living a life of freedom, potential, and possibilities in every situation!

We've all had some kind of experience where we believed that the Universe was looking out for us, or we received spiritual assistance in some way. There are those moments in time when we can see how everything fits together and say "Aha!" to the order and beauty we can see in our lives. The story of my flat tire is a vivid example of that for me.

The Dalai Lama said, "I am open to the guidance of synchronicity, and do not let expectations hinder my path." Our lives are full of expectations and rules, and it seems that by a certain age, we no longer believe in synchronicity. But just outside our window and in our everyday lives, miracles are happening. When we open up and connect with the earth, we can experience such wonder and magic every single day.

Jean Houston's Story

Not long ago I had the opportunity to drive Dr. Jean Houston from Lake Arrowhead Resort and Spa, located in the San Bernardino National Forest in California, to a nearby airport. Jean is one of the principal founders of the Human Potential Movement; a scholar, philosopher, and researcher in human capacity; and one of the foremost visionary thinkers of our time.

As we were slowly driving down the mountain, Jean told me several stories from her life. I'm sure she'd related them hundreds of times, but I hung on every word. She wasn't boastful or a name-dropper—although she's interacted with some of the most powerful people in the world, advising President and Mrs. Clinton, President and Mrs. Carter, dignitaries from the United Nations (UN), the Dalai Lama, and many more. Somehow we ended up talking about connecting to our own inner voice to help us on our life's path, and Jean told me an incredible story about the importance of paying attention to our connection with the Universe.

She prefaced the story by telling me how much she travels. She's on the go about 170 days a year, giving lectures and workshops all around the world to the UN and universities, to political and business leaders, and to those interested in improving their lives. She has worked with more than 40 cultures in 100 countries, helping them retain their own unique customs and traditions while integrating into the larger global community that is quickly emerging.

Jean said that at one point, she'd been on the road for several weeks and was supposed to deliver an address to the UN the following morning. Although she was exhausted, Jean, who came from a family of show-business executives and performers, knew that the show must go on. She always kept her commitments, no matter how tired she was. Yet on this particular night, she felt far more fatigued than usual and really wanted to go home. Every fiber of her being was telling her not to live up to her commitment in the morning. So she didn't fight it. She picked up the phone, called her contact at the UN, and told her that she wouldn't be able to speak as scheduled.

The woman pleaded with Jean to reconsider, telling her that dignitaries from all over the world were eager to see her presentation, they'd been planning the event forever, and everyone would be very disappointed if she cancelled. But Jean just knew that she *had* to go home, and there was nothing that anybody could say or do to convince her otherwise. She changed her travel arrangements, and got the last flight out of New York back to San Francisco that day. She arrived home safely, but she was so exhausted that she fell asleep as soon as she got home. The next morning she awoke to discover that the plane she would have been on had she given that talk at the UN had crashed. That plane turned out to be United Airlines Flight 93, which was en route to San Francisco on September 11, 2001.

Jean was just one person who was connected to the intelligence of the Universe on the days surrounding September 11. Many people on that dreadful day listened to their intuition or got some sort of spiritual assistance and ended up staying home, missing a train, or otherwise changing their plans.

When we're connected to ourselves and the Universe around us, then we're able to trust our inner knowing—even when it might let someone down or seem unprofessional, out of character, or unreliable. It's at that moment, when we act on instinct, that we're engaged in the interconnectedness of possibilities.

Jean hadn't understood why she'd felt so compelled to go home; it hadn't made sense professionally or personally. Yet if she hadn't trusted her heart and allowed herself to be swayed by external forces—the UN coordinator's plea, her desire to please others, or her worry about not looking professional—she would have ignored such a strong message from the Universe . . . and we know what would have happened.

When we trust that we're part of a larger Universe and act on inspired (or "in-spirit") action, then we simply trust the messages, synchronicities, and feelings that show up in our lives and are open to spiritual assistance. It doesn't mean that we just sit there and wait for our order, and it certainly doesn't mean that we have to control the process. Inspired action is about having the courage to trust our hearts—to take action based on our connection, no matter what the external evidence may be—and then trusting that the action is aligned with our highest good.

Gardens are safe places where we can discover how to connect to our inner world, to others, to the earth, and to the Universe. We learn to trust ourselves to care for the gardens through our intuition and knowing. We learn to trust nature's wisdom as we watch our seeds blossom into plants and trees. And we learn to trust the power of the Universe as we encounter more and more meaningful experiences or synchronicities during our days. When we're able to witness these truths—these miracles—in our Life Gardens and in our everyday lives, then we're on the path toward freedom.

The next seed we're going to plant is that of balance. Once we're connected to our intuition, then we can use that wisdom to bring our Life Gardens into balance.

Digging Deeper: Trust Your Vibes

When you dig deeper and connect to your intuition, you're helping your Life Garden grow with the assistance of the invisible realms of the Universe. To learn how to trust your vibes, you can:

1. Read *Trust Your Vibes: Secret Tools for Six-Sensory Living* by Sonia Choquette. Sonia is an incredible storyteller, vibrational healer, and six-sensory spiritual teacher who works with people personally and professionally. This book provides practical things to do to get in touch with your intuition, gut feelings, meaningful coincidences, or sixth sense—basically, your connection to the Universe. If you're looking to deepen your connection to the divine so that you can see the magic in life, then this is a good guide to help take you through the opening of this channel.

Intuition is important for your career, relationships, health, finances, and creative endeavors. When you work with your sixth sense, then you are guided to live your best life and are open to the spiritual assistance that awaits you. (This book also has an excellent workplace-oriented "sequel": *Trust Your Vibes at Work, and Let Them Work for You.*)

2. Keep a connection journal. It can really help you track the synchronicities, coincidences, and miracles you notice in life. Maybe you think of someone and then he or she e-mails or calls you, you seemingly bump into the person you've wanted to meet, or you get sick when you have a feeling that someone isn't on your side. When you record such events, it provides you with evidence of the role connection plays in your life.

3. Make an appointment. Seek out an intuitive counselor or healer who can talk to you about what's going on in your life. I don't mean the psychic down the street with the neon sign in the window. There are many reputable teachers, healers, and facilitators out there who don't have to advertise. Ask around and find someone you feel is a good match for you—someone you connect with personally and professionally, who is on the same wavelength and will understand you. If you're open to challenging your beliefs, then a session with a reputable healer or intuitive counselor is a good way to start opening up about how you think about the unseen. Get out of your head and start to trust your vibes!

CHAPTER SEVEN

BALANCE

"The best and safest thing is to keep
a balance in your life, acknowledge the great
powers around us and in us. If you can do that,
and live that way, you are really a wise man."

— EURIPIDES

An organic garden is a sustainable system managed by the balance of nature. This type of gardening stresses the importance of well-nourished soil, relies on plants that are native and suitable to the area, and is in alignment with all aspects of the environment to produce a vibrant and productive harvest. Although organic fruits and vegetables may not look perfect on the outside, they definitely taste better, and they're more beneficial for our health and planet.

While chemical fertilizers may create bumper crops in the short term, they also disturb the ecological harmony of any garden system. Plants are no longer so naturally pest resistant; the acidity and alkalinity of the garden gets thrown out of whack; and, ultimately, the soil becomes stripped. We're then left without the resources we need to produce even a single crop the following year—unless we resort to greater chemical interference, and greater imbalance.

Organic farmers understand the importance of a balanced, healthy ecosystem. A garden that exists in harmony with itself and everything surrounding it protects the diversity of the earth, the creatures that live there, and the richness of the soil. I find it interesting that after a season in an organic garden, the soil is better off for having produced fruit. It's a win-win situation for everybody involved: the plants, the gardener, and the planet. Organic gardening may not be the easiest choice, but chemical fertilizer is like any quick fix—it produces miraculous and instantaneous results in the short term, but then it exacts serious costs down the line.

As a kid, my friend Jason won the science fair by creating a completely harmonious and self-sustaining ecosystem. He had newts, salamanders, frogs, fish, and plants all carefully assembled into this miniature world in such a way that each species was able to meet its own needs for survival, as well as furnish essential components to the entire environment. Jason's world was so well balanced that he was able to seal his ecosystem, so it no longer required any intervention from him. He'd created an environment that could survive on its own in perpetuity.

You can try my friend's experiment yourself by taking a sealable container (such as a jar, aquarium, or bottle) and filling the bottom with a layer of pebbles and soil. Then insert some plants into the soil, spray them with a fine mist of water, add the wildlife you want to put in there, and place the container near a window for light. Close the container with a temporary seal so that you can observe the ecosystem for several weeks to ensure that it's active and alive. During those first weeks you may have to add or remove water or adjust the light source until you get the exact balance for a healthy and thriving ecosystem.

Jason won the science fair because he managed to illustrate just how critically connected every component in the environment is to everything else—when one thing is out of balance, the whole ecosystem will suffer. As his project proved, proper balance in our Life Gardens is critical to a healthy and sustainable life.

Many of us place so much emphasis on trying to have it all that we focus on one area of our Gardens at the expense of the others. We give too much of ourselves, we fixate on external results, we think we can control everything, and we're consumed with *doing*—working hard, keeping busy, and making things happen. In our struggle to keep up the pace, we keep going against the natural flow of life, which sometimes makes things very difficult. When we go with the flow, it's so easy to find ourselves in harmony with our dreams, well-being, and spirituality.

All things in a garden system are interconnected, so no one part can prosper unless everything is doing well. Just by looking at my own garden, I can tell if it's in balance or not. When I'm spending a little bit of time each day in each area of it, everything feels fresh, green, and alive—and so do I! But when I'm in the tomato patch for days, trying to force as much productivity as I can from my six plants, then the adjoining areas get overgrown with weeds and encourage pests . . . which ultimately gobble up the very tomatoes I was working so hard to achieve.

Gardens offer us some essential lessons in creating balance in our lives. If we're to thrive, we must both give and receive, work and play, relax and struggle, ascend and decline, live and die. If our lives ever feel off-kilter, all we have to do is shift our perspective to restore harmony to them. Lives, like gardens, are resilient; they'll bounce back as soon as they get the right combination of the things they need.

Giving and Receiving

One day a tabby cat suddenly appeared in my garden. As I spent time outside with my herbs, tomatoes, and begonias, I saw her quite often. When I opened the door in the morning, she'd be sunning herself on my front steps; when I looked out the back window, I'd catch her walking across the railing of my deck like a gymnast on a balance beam. The cat didn't have a collar, and no one in the neighborhood knew whom she belonged to, so I assumed that she was either abandoned or lost. She'd made her temporary home in my neck of the woods.

I thought this cat was very cute and wanted to adopt her, but she wouldn't come near me. She was obviously love deprived, so even though I adored her from the beginning—I sent love toward her, was kind to her, fed her, gave her water, and wished to stroke her fur—she didn't return the sentiment. When I did get close enough to try to pet her, she'd scratch and hiss at me and then run away. She kept resisting the love and affection she so desperately needed.

I realized that even though I was willing to give this lonely creature love, she wasn't ready to receive it yet, so I had to keep giving and wait until she *was* ready. I named her Cici and continued to offer her affection and sustenance for more than a year. Finally, she changed her belief patterns and trusted me enough to receive my love.

Like the plants that needed water in my garden, Cici served as a clear example of how we all give and receive. I believe that she desperately wanted my attention, but she had a very difficult time letting me in. She wasn't aligned with the energy of love and affection because she'd been reinforced with another type of energy altogether.

Human beings aren't much different from this cat. If we aren't getting something in our lives that we really want—such as love, money, or health—then we need to look within rather than try to control our external circumstances. We need to ask ourselves what is inside of us that is unable or unwilling to *receive* what we so desperately need. And how can we shift that energy so we can accept the love, abundance, and well-being the Universe is waiting to offer us?

Many of us think that security is primarily about financial success, but we know from tragedies we've witnessed or experienced that money and belongings can be gone in an instant. *Currency,* our word for money, is derived from the Latin word that means "to run" or "to flow." That is, it's just another form of energy or exchange that runs through our lives. Yet our society is so focused on fast results, making a quick buck, and greed that these beliefs about money have disrupted the natural flow of currency energy in the world. The result has been a swell of negative energy in the masses, who react by hoarding cash and possessions and still constantly feel deprived. This mind-set is not in alignment with the natural order of the Universe, which is balance and abundance.

Most people who are trying to cultivate a life that matters will find themselves challenged in the area of money. I'm no exception. Ever since I was a child, I have always been able to make money and was very fortunate to get high-paying jobs. I never worried about money until I planted the Seeds of Freedom. As I worked on other parts of my Life Garden, my financial security became challenged. However, since I wanted to realize what I'd planned for my entire Garden, I was committed to moving through this.

I was dedicated to my personal and spiritual transformation, but I still needed money to pay the bills. In fact, it had gotten to the point that I didn't know how I was going to make my mortgage payment the next month. So, during my meditations, I started to sincerely ask the Universe for assistance in this area. I asked for a consulting project, the sale of my house, a winning lottery ticket, or any kind of windfall. I'd never been in this situation before, so I surrendered to the Universe for support in helping me receive.

Around this time there was a conference in Chicago I wanted to attend, but I obviously didn't have the funds to pay for the registration. I'd offered to trade services or work at the event in exchange for attending, but the organizers weren't interested in that type of situation. Even so, I kept the conference on my calendar and trusted that somehow I'd get there.

Several weeks later, one of the organizers called me about something I was working on. She then said that I needed to be at this conference and asked if I minded writing an article for the industry trade magazine in exchange for attending the event. Did I mind? I was going to get to attend the conference! And it turned out to be everything I had anticipated. I could feel the presenters' and participants' excitement and enthusiasm, and I learned a lot. I also met some great people, including a woman named Maxine.

Maxine was going to be in Atlanta the following week, and she asked if I'd join her for dinner at the Buckhead Diner, a local favorite. I didn't hesitate to say yes. I was really looking forward to spending more time with her to discuss how to bring consciousness to business, and how to help people achieve more freedom in their lives . . . at least that's what I thought the dinner was going to be about.

Maxine and I started our conversation with small talk about the conference, Atlanta, and some other points of mutual interest. Then the mood abruptly shifted when she unexpectedly asked, "Tell me, Heather, what do you need?"

"What?" I replied, somewhat befuddled. Nobody had ever asked me something like this at a business meeting.

"What do you need?" she asked again. "I'm getting the sense that you're in need of something right now, and I want to help you."

"Well, I could really use your help on a project I've been thinking of." I started to explain the project, but then she interrupted me.

"Do you have trouble receiving?" she asked.

"Well, I guess I must," I said.

Maxine continued to talk about how she was listening to her intuition—she was being guided to ask me about what I needed, as well as to help me out. I began to tear up as I explained my financial situation and my anxiety about paying the mortgage that month. I told her that I'd never been in any kind of financial trouble before, and I was unsure how to get out of it.

On the spot, Maxine offered me a $5,000 interest-free loan that I could repay when I was back on my feet. It was difficult for me to receive this, but I did so because it was coming from an authentic place in both of our hearts. My prayers to the Universe had been answered. And I didn't just get a much-needed loan from this experience—I was also given the lesson that when any of us are willing and able to receive as well as give, the Universe provides us with everything we need. When we're open to the flow of life, we can be open to surprises like this one.

A week earlier, Maxine didn't even exist in my consciousness. When I thought about how I was going to pay my mortgage, this option certainly wasn't up for consideration. But because I was open to receiving—first, the invitation to go to the conference; then the invitation to dinner; and finally, the financial assistance—I was able to make my mortgage payment. The Universe works in mysterious and beautiful ways.

Real security is an inside job first, and then we make it solid and concrete in our external world. We must discover if material possessions actually give us security, or if it's a grounded sense of self that makes us feel safer.

Most of us have physical bank accounts with money in them. Although we don't actually have a pile of cash that we can touch, we believe the numbers on a sheet of paper that say we have access to those funds in the accounts we've set up. Yet our money can only take us so far—what we're really looking for in life are the intangibles, such as peace, love, and joy. How can we measure such things? Where do we go during the storms of life? In our Life Gardens, we don't measure our success with cash, titles, or power; rather, we look at significance, meaning, and beauty. If we haven't been developing the spiritual parts of our Gardens, then our roots in this area aren't deep, and we don't have the strength to endure any of the challenges we might face.

When you know how to freely give and receive, then you're allowing abundance to continue to flow in the Universe and in your life. However, if you block it, it affects the natural course of the entire ecosystem. So if you want to learn how to receive, affirm that you are open to doing so and focus on being thankful. If you don't already appreciate what you have, then how can you expect more abundance to come into your life? Cultivate an attitude of gratitude and you'll be opening your Life Garden to receiving more abundance in all areas.

Life and Death

In a vegetable garden, we constantly see endings and beginnings and births and deaths—all of which are welcomed as organic and necessary parts of the life cycle. But in our own lives, many of us have a very difficult time acknowledging that anything has to end.

If someone we know passes away—or a career path, relationship, or dream is over—we try to avoid confronting the inevitable. We tend to ignore the fact that we've suffered a loss, and neglect to give ourselves the time we need to acknowledge the sacredness of endings, which are as crucial as beginnings in the cycle of our Life Gardens. Even the structures of most companies support this. Most businesses give six weeks for maternity leave, but only three days off to tend to the death of a loved one.

As I was cultivating my own Garden, I experienced many deaths: the loss of an identity at work; the end of a deep, loving relationship; broken dreams; and the deterioration of friendships as I began to change and grow. In my physical garden, I accepted that endings were a natural part of the process, but that didn't cross over into my own life. Somehow I wanted to keep everything alive and didn't want anything to end. This realization pushed me to examine many of my fears and deep-seated beliefs.

I soon realized that endings are so difficult because we feel lost without the old and haven't yet started the new—and many of us are uncomfortable with this in-between place. And death brings on a whole set of fears about living a life that matters. We start asking ourselves, "Does what we do even mean anything? What happens when we die? Do we go on after death?"

When we're more intimate with death—when we're more aware of the harmony of the entire ecosystem of existence—then we see life and death as natural, organic, and inextricable parts of the same cycle. A garden teaches us that the earth has to remain fallow for a period so that new plants can spring forth the next year. I feel that we need to be less afraid of our lives ending, and more afraid that they'll never actually begin.

Since I've been planting the Seeds of Freedom in my life, I've completely lost my fear of death and endings. I'm no longer afraid to transition to another state, nor am I fearful of my loved ones dying. (It's not that I won't be sad, it's just that I know I won't fall apart.) We all come into this world the same way, and we all exit the same way. None of us can escape it.

We often keep so busy with our day-to-day tasks that we don't spend a lot of time addressing the real issues regarding the meaning of life and death. We need to talk about, and at least try to understand this subject, because the acceptance of death and endings will free us from the paralyzing fear of the unknown.

We must remember that we are all energy from the same source. Since energy can't be created or destroyed, in death we just transition to another form, or a new season in the garden.

If you don't know how to see loss as part of the balance between endings and beginnings, and you're still very attached to someone or something you've lost, you'll never be able to let another person or experience in. It's as if you're carrying a huge weight on your back as you go through life.

Giving yourself permission to just be with your grief will allow you to feel the emotions and then create the environment to heal. If you fear death, you must embrace life—breathe more of it into your Garden so that you can access the emotions associated with death.

It might seem that keeping yourself busy with projects and activities is the way to move forward, but this will actually repress your feelings and push them deeper into your cellular system. This will make healing more difficult as the emotions will compress and become more intense. The pressure will build, and that weight you're carrying will become even heavier. Believe it or not, it's much easier to acknowledge and feel your emotions instead of pushing them aside.

Runa Bouius's Story

I met Runa at the Conscious Capitalism Institute conference at Bentley University in Boston a few years ago, and we've been friends ever since. Her perspective on the role of life and death is very inspiring and something I wanted to share.

Western culture places a stigma on death and dying, so sometimes we forget that it is simply natural and unavoidable. A native of Iceland, Runa sees death and dying happening to us all the time in the form of changes, endings, or closures of one sort or another. Think of ending a marriage or relationship, finishing a long-term project, leaving a colleague, changing careers or retiring, moving to a new place, going through a financial meltdown, or watching the kids go off to college. Some of these changes are welcomed and self-selected; others are thrown at us without warning.

Runa has gone through many of these life changes herself. For example, in 1994 she chose to sell the retail store and the importing and wholesale company she owned in Reykjavík, leaving behind a very successful career of 20 years in the world of cosmetics and perfumes. This was a death process that she invited into her life. However, death also visited her in another form when her husband unexpectedly passed away. In an instant, both her career and marriage were gone.

My friend decided to leave Iceland and move to the United States in pursuit of new beginnings. So, in addition to losing her husband and her identity as a successful businesswoman, she was also separating from her family, co-workers, friends, and community. She was leaving everything she'd ever identified with, except being a mom. She flew over the Atlantic Ocean with her two young sons and a few suitcases to start her new life, moving toward a new vision in a foreign land. Many people in Runa's shoes may have been terribly afraid, but she was brimming with excitement.

The girl from Reykjavík settled in Santa Fe, New Mexico. There, she started a business, met a nice man, and created a new life that was very exciting for her. Her Life Garden was flourishing in all areas. And then, after 14 wonderful years, Runa found herself in the midst of another kind of death. Her boys had gone off to start their own lives, her healing and apprentice work in Santa Fe seemed complete, and she felt a pull to be on the West Coast. Runa's inner knowing told her that it was time to go through another passage. Consequently, she and her longtime partner split up, and in the middle of all this change and unrest, her beloved father passed away in Iceland.

She left behind the familiar again—her friends and community; her cat, Fleygur; and her beautiful home—and moved to Los Angeles. She was challenged to start anew even as she mourned the death of two of the most important relationships in her life: the one she had with her father, and the one she had with her lover. This was yet another reminder of the unexpected and unforeseen, which Runa embraced.

People often tell her, "You're so courageous," or "How can you be so brave?" But she doesn't see it that way. Rather, she views death as part of living. She allows her old self to die when it needs to, and rejoices in the birth of a new self (usually an upgraded version) from the deep sea of her soul. When she allows that death to happen, she honors the authentic relationship she has with herself and the Universe, and trusts how it wants to express itself in the world.

My wise friend understands that completions and endings are natural and sacred parts of living. She starts every new cycle with intense excitement and an infectious zest for life. She sees every ending and beginning as part of the never-ending spiral of life that comes from deep within herself. She is absolutely in balance.

Joy and sadness are part of the natural flow of life. When we let ourselves just be with any emotion, then we're demonstrating that we're able to go with the flow—and we feel more powerful, complete, and open for future experiences. We never know what will emerge in our rebirth, but that's the exciting part. Like Runa, we usually discover an upgraded, wiser, or more complete version of ourselves.

Obviously, when you've confronted a significant loss in your life, it's not a joyful experience, but it *is* part of the journey. If you handle the situation so that it doesn't become a roadblock to growing a thriving and beautiful Life Garden, that will make all the difference. When you're able to see the situation, feel your emotion, focus on the positive impacts that the person or experience had on your life, and then move through it, your Life Garden can flourish. You'll be able to continue on your journey, grateful for all you've gone through. If you can maintain a positive outlook and a stronger knowing that you can handle loss gracefully—with courage and a loving perspective—then you'll be able to stay in balance.

Doing and Being

We are very good "doers." Our society is about accomplishing, achieving, and getting things done; and we value action, hard work, and activity. The world is certainly full of exciting opportunities, but we've created our own limitations and disabling beliefs that we have to make things happen.

Balance comes from just being, which is what your soul craves. When you start to explore this idea further, it's going to feel uncomfortable at first—you'll feel as if you're not working hard enough or learning enough. Therefore, it's important to remember that when you decided to plant the Seeds of Freedom, the rules changed. *You are enough, without doing anything at all.*

When you're aligned with what is right for you, you're living in harmony with your own integrity and authenticity. Therefore, it doesn't matter what's happening on the outside—the only thing that matters is that you stay true to yourself. You need to be gentle and kind with yourself first and know that your best is enough. Your value in life comes from who you are, not what you do or what you have. Don't compare your Life Garden to anyone else's because it will never make you feel good. You don't know the depths of energy in other people. You don't know their truth, experiences, or values. What you see on the surface is not always reality.

In the Eastern philosophy of Taoism, there is a term called *wu-wei,* which means "to do by not doing." This is something that most Westerners don't understand—we live in such an action-oriented society, built on the sturdiness of the Protestant work ethic, that not doing is underappreciated. According to the Taoists, wu-wei is necessary to help us achieve a harmonious state of being in which our actions are in alignment with the ebb and flow of the world. Like the lapping of waves on the beach, there is effortlessness, an ease, a trust, and an awareness in this belief that allows us to go with the flow and take inspired action.

For lots of us, the most difficult part of working with our Life Gardens is letting go of control. We're so accustomed to managing every detail, meeting endless deadlines, and making things happen that handing over power to an unseen energy source will feel really uncomfortable at first. But if we can surrender and go with the flow, then things are going to go very smoothly. It's when we try to fight the process that life becomes difficult. (Think of the difference between paddling a kayak upstream and downstream.)

Whenever you try to control a situation, you're just working harder in your attempt to keep everything together. You're going against the natural growth and flow of life. But if you can learn to walk away and not engage in something that bothers you, you're allowing the Universe to restore harmony. Remember, everyone is working together, so learn to let go and objectively watch what happens around you. You'll be free to see the magic.

Once you can detach, then it's much easier to go with the flow. You know that the outcome will always be in your favor and is aligned with the highest good of all involved. It also makes the journey that much easier, as you're being carried by the current of energy and not pushing up against it. Life can then unfold with ease, grace, and fun!

When you're in balance, your head and heart are integrated. You can't stay in your logical mind all the time. It's really good to educate yourself as much as you can, but you also need to use the power of your heart and intuition that you've been learning about in the last few chapters. When you're in balance, you might use your intellect to make a decision—but then you check in with your inner knowing to make sure that it's the *right* decision. And when your head and heart are aligned, you can stay in the moment and truly focus on what's at hand.

In a world where multitasking is so prized, it may feel very strange to slow down and pay attention to just one thing at a time. But if you can do so, you'll be able to transform each moment of your life. In college, I read psychologist Mihaly Csikszentmihalyi's book *Flow: The Psychology of Optimal Experience,* and I found it fascinating. The author discovered that when our attention is totally engaged in one thing—such as painting, creating a delicious meal, solving a problem, or working on a project—the ego falls away. Time flies. Every action, movement, and thought inevitably follows from the previous one like a jazz improvisation; our whole being is involved, and we're using our skills to the utmost. Focus and flow produce intense feelings of joy and rapture. When we're in the flow, we feel as if we're one with the entire world. It feels like an altered state of consciousness.

When we're able to perceive the wholeness in our lives—to see the possibilities and become one with them through activities that take us to a "flow" state—then it's not just about us anymore. The sense of separateness that we feel from other people, the environment, or the Universe disappears and we can tap into all possibilities. We then have the opportunity to integrate this feeling of bliss, of oneness, into everything we do. We are in balance with the world.

The Ins and Outs of Breathing

Our breath is what connects us with all living things on the planet, especially our gardens. In fact, all the plants in our ecosystem, particularly the trees and forests, are like the lungs of Earth that take in our carbon dioxide and provide us with the precious oxygen that we need to survive.

Breath is the only thing that separates us from death; it's literally the air that fills us with life. When we can't breathe, we're stifling our life or trying to control it. Did you ever notice that when you're afraid, you hold your breath? Simply focusing on your breath can have a calming effect on your mind and emotions. Breathing is a way to release your troubles. No matter what the situation, it will help bring balance back to you immediately.

We can't be present for ourselves or others if we're not present in the moment. Breath keeps us in the moment, and is the bridge to our consciousness; breath gives us freedom. Yet somehow, most of us have lost touch with this natural rhythm—we're breathing from the neck up. Deeply inhaling and exhaling will help us get in touch with the energy locked in our bodies, and then it will free up that energy for the growth and expansion of our being.

How do you breathe? Are your breaths long or short, shallow or deep, tight or expansive? Think of babies with their big belly breaths. Adults, on the other hand, are shallow breathers because we've been taught to suppress our emotions. When we don't express our emotions, then this energy gets blocked in our bodies and trapped at a cellular level. Energy has to go somewhere, so after it's been held hostage in the body, it usually comes out as some kind of disease. Breathing is essential to good health and well-being. If our breathing is shallow, then so is our life—yet this connection usually goes unnoticed.

Breathing is the "flowing of spirit" to you and through you; it links you to your energy source and will help you gain the strength to live more courageously. Breathing brings your attention back to yourself and the present moment.

You can also use your breath to pause a moment and connect to your feelings so that you can bring balance back to yourself. You may not feel comfortable with "the pause," but give it a try because it will add dimension to your life. Before you do something big, take a moment to breathe so that you're totally present, in your body and in the moment. When you do, you may see and feel things that are beyond the five senses. Pausing allows you to regroup, focus on what's important, and see what's really going on. Your breath is your life energy, and pausing enables you to pay attention to that energy. When you take in more breath and take time to pause, you have more energy. Life is more robust, and you're even happier.

There are a lot of ways in which you can practice the power of breathing. The next time you're sitting in traffic or stuck in a meeting that's driving you nuts, place your hand on your belly and take some deep breaths. No one will know what you're doing, and it will immediately help you feel calmer and take your mind off the traffic jam or the annoying co-worker. You can also use this technique when you're going to sleep. Breathe in the positive—focus on love, abundance, and the like—and as you exhale, release anything negative, such as tension, stress, or worry.

Conscious breathing is calming, connects you with yourself, and helps you make decisions from love instead of fear. Your creativity and productivity increase when your body is enjoying a stress-free life, and you're free to just be. You're more able to access the flow, you're happier, and you enjoy a natural high from the release of feel-good chemicals. This type of breathing also stops the mind from allowing your emotions to spiral down. Your breath and emotions are intertwined, just like your body and mind are. All of your emotions are followed by different kinds of breath, be it sobbing, laughing, squeals of joy, or sighs of relief.

What is your breathing saying about you right now? Are you laughing or sighing? Are you excited or sobbing? Find out what inspires you, what brings you joy, what you find beautiful, and what stirs your soul—and then just sit quietly and appreciate the glory of whatever it is. You'll gain mental clarity whenever you connect to your breath and spirit.

If you want to be powerful in life, then you need to know how to control your breath. The breath comes and goes, thoughts and ideas come and go, sensations in the body come and go, and your awareness to your connection comes and goes. You need to observe your life the same way. Everything comes and goes . . . everything is in balance.

Exercise: **Breathing Techniques**

Here's how you can learn to bring awareness and balance to any situation. Conscious breathing helps you become aware of how you're feeling, and lets you know if you have any unwanted tension in your body. You can practice your technique using the following steps:

1. Sit up straight in a chair, close your eyes, and place your hands over your belly.

2. Inhale and feel your belly filling with air. Make sure your abdominal muscles are relaxed.

3. Once you feel as if your belly is full, keep inhaling. The goal is to fill the middle of your chest so that your chest and rib-cage area expand.

4. Pause and hold your breath for just a moment, and then begin to slowly and evenly exhale, like a tire losing air.

5. Relax your chest and rib cage and begin to tighten your abdominal muscles to force out the remaining air.

6. Continue to relax your mind and just focus on your breathing.

7. Practice this exercise for five minutes.

Planting the seed of balance in your Life Garden means that you are coming into your wholeness. You are bringing all aspects of yourself to your awareness—in mind, body, and spirit—and are able to flow with the ups and downs of life. Balance is about knowing what's right for you and surrendering to the energy in your life. When you're tapped into the energy source that is within and around you, then you can live in alignment with that source energy. And that's when you have the freedom to grow in perfect balance, just like all living things in the ecosystem can. You'll be able to thrive naturally and organically without trying so hard, without the need for anything artificial in the world. You'll be able to experience the moments in life that really matter.

When you're in balance, you bring that characteristic to all you do. You have freedom in knowing that your life is one of authenticity and alignment. You don't have to work so hard, and everything is easy and natural. You're living from a place of integrity in all that you do—all parts of your Life Garden are working together for the greater good. When you're in balance in your Garden, you're true to all parts of yourself—no matter what your life partner, children, friends, or business colleagues want you to do. When you're in balance, you have good timing and are not motivated by results. You're free to flow with the changes in life, knowing that everything will be reborn the following season.

When you become whole, then you have the power to create, nourish, and transform your life. You find your wholeness through the delicate balance of giving and receiving, living and dying, and doing and being. You are also able to embrace both your feminine and masculine energies. A balanced Life Garden means that all areas of your life are feeding and contributing to one another. You're free to go with the flow; and this allows you to see opportunities, reduce the number of conflicts, and expand and evolve because you're partnering with the laws of nature and the Universe.

In this chapter, you learned the importance of giving and receiving, life and death, and doing and being. You now know that when you're in balance, you're able to handle the constant stream of changes in life with ease and flow. The next chapter is about planting the seed of clearing. Once you can identify the boulders in your Life Garden, you'll be able to clear them out to allow for future growth.

Digging Deeper: DoBeDoBeDo

To dig deeper and understand the delicate balance of your Life Garden, you can:

1. Just be. Remember the Frank Sinatra song "Strangers in the Night"? If so, you may recall that at the end, he sings, "DoBe-DoBeDo." Like most crooners in his day, Sinatra was ad-libbing or "scatting" parts of the song. He wasn't trying to make it perfect; he was making it his own. He just went with the flow of the music and sang something that turned out to be pretty catchy. Think about this lyric when you're doing too much or trying too hard. It's time to bring your Life Garden into balance and stop "do-do-doing" and add some "being" to your life.

2. Watch the DVD *The Living Matrix* **by Greg Becker and Harry Massey.** This film presents some exciting ideas about healing, our medical system, and the nature of human health. This feature-length film documents leading-edge scientists and doctors who are revealing new ways of treating illness and promoting wellness. I highly recommend this movie to learn more about alternatives available so that you can then integrate your own wellness practices based on what's right for you.

3. Do the work in the book *You Can Heal Your Life* **by Louise Hay.** If you're willing to dig deeper and really do some intense work that will help bring true healing and wellness to your life, then this book is for you. It's full of exercises that help you identify your limiting beliefs, change your thinking, and improve the quality of your life. It's been a life changer for many people I know, and it can help with anything from relationship issues to work concerns. When you heal your life and bring balance to your body, then your Life Garden flourishes.

CHAPTER EIGHT

CLEARING

"As you become more clear about who
you really are, you'll be better able to decide
what is best for you—the first time around."

— OPRAH WINFREY

As I started spending more time in Hilton Head and really attended to my Life Garden, I felt the need to plant a real one there as well. I thought it would be a good idea to create a *community* garden, since it would give me a wonderful opportunity to both meet my neighbors and enjoy some organic produce. I also thought that the ideal place for this would be an area down by an unused tennis court. Although the court itself was functional, it wasn't very nice to look at.

It was, however, plopped in the middle of the woods. It was surrounded by large oaks with Spanish moss draped on the limbs, towering pines, palm trees, bamboo, jasmine, and some other kind of vine that took over most of the tree limbs in the midst of summer. The ground was covered with fallen leaves; broken branches; and smatterings of ivy, hosta, and some wild ferns. Yet it was mostly the playground for the large variety of birds, squirrels, and the occasional alligator scurrying about and enjoying the natural setting.

There were two small patches filled with overgrown bushes at the entrance to the tennis court that hadn't been touched in years. The soil had been neglected, was hard and crusty, and needed a lot of work to make it worthy of planting anything. I would need to clear out a lot of dead bushes, prune back some overgrown trees, weed between the pavers, and put up some boundaries to designate the garden area.

Gardens often require clearing—either to prepare land for new plants, to get ready for the winter months, or to just do the normal maintenance that is needed to keep them free of uninvited guests. Clearing is about looking around and getting rid of what you don't want so that you can easily grow what you *do* want. It's always a win-win for both you and the garden—and often for an entire community.

To that end, our shared garden in Hilton Head now enhances the beautiful wooded landscape that changes color with the seasons. For example, we currently have some azaleas and rhododendrons that bloom pink and purple in the springtime, and plenty of fresh fruits and veggies in the summer. That tennis court has the most beautiful surroundings I can imagine, and it brought so many of us together in the process. The end result was well worth the effort.

Clear Your Field for New Growth

Most of us in the West place little value on the person who has an obvious intention and a lot of integrity. But in our Life Gardens, it's crucial that we are clear about what we want and focus on our own authenticity and alignment.

In our society, people have made money God and success the Almighty, but this is not the truth of life. Success is determined by how we feel; it's having a life that is aligned with what we want and what we love doing. Success is about listening to our intuition and following it, even when it doesn't make sense. It means that if everyone is going right and we hear that we're supposed to go left, we need to go left. As we change our focus from an outer one (money, titles, and appearance) to an inner one (integrity, truth, and compassion), there will always be challenges. When we plant our Gardens, for instance, we may say that we want spiritual assistance—but if we aren't tending to our inner landscapes, then it's akin to wanting the phone to ring when the line is busy. We need to clear the line if we're truly going to co-create our Gardens with the help of the Universe. If we have a sincere willingness to change our lives and get rid of the unwanted, then we will absolutely be given the opportunity and support to grow what's best for us.

In order to have flourishing Life Gardens, our inner and outer landscapes need to match. In other words, we won't be able to have a million dollars in the bank until we believe that we're worthy of receiving that sum of money. And we can't plant the seeds for having a family until we can nourish our own needs. We have to clear our fields of any emotional blocks and be open to a deep connection with *all* parts of ourselves.

How we interpret our lives is directly associated with how we interpret our experiences emotionally. We either see ourselves as worthy or unworthy, healthy or sick, a success or a failure, lovable or unlovable, hopeful or desperate. The way we feel about ourselves is locked in an emotional system: it's tied in to our thoughts, feelings, and physical bodies; our connection to the spiritual part of ourselves; and the actions we take in our environment.

Regardless of education, race, gender, or economic status, most of us have some kind of block that's holding us back. These blocks tend to be subconscious, created in our bodies to alleviate or withstand any pain we've experienced—be it emotional anguish from financial loss, failure, rejection, betrayal, resentment, shame, or fear; or physical ailments suffered from disease or abuse. These memories are stored in our bodies and poison the ground for any new thoughts, feelings, or actions that want to take root. Or you might be harboring a secret that continues to grow bigger and bigger with each passing year.

I believe that we all are enough and essentially whole as we are; we have the potential to be, do, or have anything we want in life.

Each of us just has different rocks, roots, pests, and weeds to get rid of. Whether we realize it or not, we have hang-ups, traumas, or beliefs that are filling our Life Gardens with environmental, mental, emotional, physical, and spiritual clutter. This clutter prevents us from moving forward and growing what we really want to harvest from our Gardens.

Since we haven't done the proper pruning and weeding or put up the right boundaries to protect what we've planted over the years, that clutter may have hit the critical point. It doesn't matter if we keep encountering a fear of success, a sense of unworthiness, post-traumatic stress, or the feeling that we're just doing the same old thing over and over again—the solution is the same. We need to clear our field to make room for new growth.

Clearing the field is hard work. It takes courage and willingness to dig up entire Gardens, if necessary, in order to examine them from the ground up and take responsibility for what we find there. Once we dig up the dirt, we know what we're dealing with and can do something about it. It doesn't matter what seeds we sow—if our patch of land is strewn with negativity, toxic waste, or huge boulders, the soil can never foster growth or produce the Gardens of our dreams.

Samantha's Story

Samantha, a prospective client, called me in tears because she'd been let go from her third job in four years. She had been given just six weeks' severance and didn't have much in savings. Her skills as an office manager were good, but they were limited—and conducting a job search in the middle of one of the worst recessions in history was difficult for her emotionally, mentally, and physically.

This woman seemed to be struggling in all areas of her Life Garden: her security was unstable, her health was failing, her relationships weren't what she desired, and her creative expression was nonexistent. Her Garden seemed to be floundering instead of flowering.

We began our sessions by exploring the Life Garden concept in detail. First, Samantha had to give herself permission to dream about her ideal Garden. Then I suggested a program of nourishing herself regularly with good food, plenty of water, and sea-salt baths so that she'd be healthy enough to plant that Garden. These simple acts helped her regain some balance in her life. She also practiced giving and receiving with friends, spent time in quiet prayer, and took a walk in nature each day.

My client was starting to feel more secure and even hopeful about her situation. And then one day she got a very negative and critical e-mail from a recruiter . . . and this blew away the calm we'd been carefully cultivating in her Garden for weeks.

Samantha had interviewed for a job that she really wanted, and the recruiter told her that she wasn't a good fit for the open position—and that the employer thought my client was "trying too hard." On any other day, this kind of feedback after an interview would have been okay, but today Samantha was feeling particularly vulnerable because she was still growing new roots in her Life Garden. So this somewhat insignificant e-mail became very significant to my client. The recruiter's comments threw her into a state of panic, and it seemed like yet another cruel blow from out of the blue.

This situation ultimately allowed Samantha to clear her field. In the process, she identified a huge boulder in her Garden: that of not being good enough. The recruiter's e-mail—which initially turned my client's life upside down—ended up helping her remove the blocks in her life so that she could plant what she wanted.

Instead of trying harder to please the hiring company or responding to this e-mail defensively, Samantha and I did some internal work first. We spent some time digging up the dirt in her Garden to find out the reason behind her insecure feelings. It turns out that up until this point, she'd spent years trying to fit in both personally and professionally. When we identified this boulder of unworthiness in her Garden, all of her problems began to make sense.

> Samantha understood that what was happening to her "out there" was actually due to what she'd planted "in here." She hadn't before realized that her subconscious thoughts and negative beliefs had been creating her external reality. Consequently, we were able to put a plan in place to help her genuinely feel worthy, to understand that she was enough and didn't have to fit a particular mold. She was able to clear away this obstacle and focus on feeling worthy and expecting more from life . . . and then receive it with open arms.

Rocks that need to be removed, brush that needs pruning, or weeds that need to be plucked from our Life Gardens all show up in the form of an unplanned expense, the end of a relationship, the rejection from a recruiter, or the like. The only way we can clear out these nuisances and let our seeds grow is by getting in there and doing some work. Yet we also need to be gentle with ourselves and spend time in our Gardens to just observe what's going on. We're all struggling with something, and I believe that we're doing our best in every situation. But when we go into our Gardens, then we can focus on what we want and how we want to feel.

If we aren't where we want to be in life, then we probably have some kind of obstacle in our Gardens that needs to be cleared away. Some of the most common ones that my clients confront are: fear of success; fear of failure; lack of self-worth; lack of abundance; or feeling unlovable, inadequate, or undeserving. Our natural state is one of success, but these limiting and deep-rooted obstructions can block us from our true selves—who are in a state of love, peace, success, abundance, and freedom.

What patterns do you see in your life? Do you continually witness the same scenario playing over and over? Do you keep getting into the same financial predicament? Do you let your boss treat you poorly? Do you find yourself in controlling relationships? Do you put your kids' needs before your own? Do you settle for less than optimal health? Do you stifle your creativity?

Once you decide to really examine what's going on in your Life Garden, look around and note where you're out of balance. What do you need to break up in the Garden? What do you need to clear away?

In your journal, write down the answers to the following questions for each area of your Garden: *security, health and wellness, vocation, relationships,* and *creative expression:*

- Is what you planted in your Garden actually growing?

- Are your values and beliefs reflected here?

- Do you have purpose and meaning in your life?

- Are you being authentic?

- Are you doing the necessary inner work to clear out any obstacles in this area?

- Do you feel as if what you are doing matters?

If you answered *no* to any of these questions, then you need to clear that area of your Garden and make some room for new growth. When you're honest with yourself, then you can dig deeper and clear out any of the weeds or rocks that are lurking there. You might not see them at first glance, but if you aren't growing the kinds of things you want, then there may indeed be problems beneath the surface.

It takes time to uncover anything that's blocking your growth. You just need to stay in alignment with what you need. So if you dig a little deeper, what do you find? As with the previous set of questions, in your journal write down the answers to the following ones for each area of your Garden:

- How do you feel?

- Do you see new growth from seeds that you planted in your vision? What does it look like?

- What doubts and obstacles do you observe?

- Do you see any recurring problems?

- What messages are you hearing?

- What inspires you here?

- What scares you here?

- What emotions rise to the surface?

- When you uncover a new layer, what do you see that was hiding beneath the surface? Do you have any secrets or unresolved fears lurking there?

- Can you pull back the layer easily, or is it difficult to do so?

When you identify and understand the unwanted things in your Life Garden, the things that cause you pain, you can put a plan together to remove them so that you have room to grow what you desire. And as you shift your attention to clearing your inner landscape, then you will start to detect shifts in your life. Your Garden will change—you'll see that different people show up, you'll be able to grow different things, and you'll be able to create different experiences.

Emotional Boulders

If you aren't telling the truth about your life and emotions, then it's a good bet that you're feeling overwhelmed or ready to explode. And since you're not allowing your feelings to flow through you, you're pushing them into your physical body—which can often result in chronic health conditions, addictions, emotional instability, or mental anguish.

Emotions are an incredible gift to let you know how you're doing. When you feel good, then you are aligned with your true self, your soul self, and you are on the path to freedom. But emotional boulders in your Garden can prevent you from growing the seeds you planted in your Life Garden.

Here are some common emotional boulders that may be buried in your garden:

— **Anger.** This is a fiery emotion filled with hate, resentment, irritability, and frustration. When you're angry, you're holding on to pain that doesn't belong to you. Ask yourself what you're angry about: Boundaries? Control? Fear? Neglect?

— **Depression.** When you're depressed, you feel a loss of empowerment, and your vital life-force energy has stopped. In short, you feel hopeless. In order to access your power again, you need to go deep within to light your flame.

— **Fear.** This is an emotion that's either paralyzing or fueling your aggression. Fear is represented by shallow breath, which blocks your energy, and it can also enhance your intuition. So what are you afraid of? Notice what you fear and how you respond. Do you want to fight or flee?

— **Grief.** Grief is caused by a lost connection to someone or something important to you. It might be the end of a friendship, the loss of a job, a divorce, a child going to college, or the death of a loved one. It might even be the death of a younger version of you, an old belief system, or dreams that never came true.

— **Guilt.** Guilt is caused by feeling bad about your actions and the failure to meet others' standards. It happens because of the gap between what you think you should do and what actually occurred. Guilt is about what others think, and it encourages you to try to please others and pulls you away from what you really want.

— **Rage.** This is an unspoken emotion. Having rage doesn't mean that you're going to act on it and hurt someone, but you still need to honor it. You may feel victimized by the way someone treated you or by something that happened to you.

— **Shame.** Shame is a condition of humiliating disgrace. It's personal and tends to lead to isolation, inferiority, depression, and alienation. Shame keeps you trapped in your own fear of being wrong and causes you to avoid feeling your real emotions.

There are no bad or wrong emotions. They're all healthy, but it's what you do with them that matters. When you block your emotions, you're essentially cutting yourself off from your energy source—from your inspiration, love, and freedom.

Your job is to learn how to deal with these feelings and take responsibility for your own life so that you can release these boulders from your Garden.

But when you're nourishing yourself, you feel your emotions. Try drinking some water, meditating, taking a sea-salt bath, screaming into a pillow, lying down in the fetal position, rubbing your belly, or just breathing into what you're feeling and letting out a good cry.

As the emotions move through your emotional body, you'll be releasing them from your physical body as well.

Exercise: Clearing Emotional Boulders

If you're willing to see what's underneath the surface, go deep inside yourself and understand why you continue to repeat the same patterns over and over; by doing so, you're taking the first step to removing a block. To help release these behaviors, grab your journal and do the following process (you can also use the chart in this exercise to help you visually see the blocks in your Life Garden):

1. **Behavior.** Look closely at each section of your Life Garden—*security, health and well-being, vocation, relationships,* and *creative expression.* If you're not bearing the fruit of what you want in each area, then it's time to identify the behavior that you see as the biggest obstacle to achieving it. Think back to your childhood to identify when you started this behavior.

2. **Benefit.** Dig deep to see what benefit you're getting from that negative behavior. If you keep doing something, then you must be receiving some benefit from it. Imagine the whiny kid getting extra attention from an adult, the jobless friend who always gets sympathy from others, or the ill parent who gets taken care of by his or her children. (This may feel like a twisted exercise, but if you're true to yourself, you can identify the benefit you get from a particular behavior.)

3. **Emotions.** How does this behavior make you feel? List out the emotions, and spend some time feeling them.

4. **Clear Plan.** Accept the behavior and emotions as a part of you—knowing that you're doing the best you can do—and gently get to work and clear out the behavior. Dig it out, prune it back, weed it out, or start to set new boundaries. Be gentle with yourself as you go through this work. Forgive yourself and anyone else involved, and let it go. Remember that you're clearing your field to allow new behaviors, new experiences, and new ways of being.

Here's an example of what you might write down:

Behavior	Benefit	Emotions	Clear Plan
Security: I never have enough money.	People take care of me.	Embarrassment Fear	I will clear the fear by challenging some beliefs about money.
Health and well-being: I eat and drink too much.	It numbs my pain.	Rage Unworthiness	I will clear out the rage by connecting with the part of me that's in pain. I can release the rage in a healthy way by screaming into a towel or throwing a temper tantrum. (Note: This is sensitive energy, and you may want to get professional help.)
Vocation: I'm always passed up for promotions.	I am safe from failing.	Unworthiness Weakness	I will clear my feelings of unworthiness by saying daily affirmations of self-love.
Relationships: I manipulate my wife to serve my needs.	I can't get hurt. I feel like I'm in control.	Feeling unlovable Fear	I will clear the air and be honest about my feelings or what I want. I will then see what happens.
Creative expression: I don't paint anymore.	I don't have to feel the pain of my childhood.	Anger Resentment	I will clear the anger by confronting my mother in a visualization and saying, "I'm angry. I have the right to be angry. I'm giving you back your anger."

Clearing is one of the most difficult seeds to plant because it requires you to be completely honest and authentic. Many people are holding on to the rage and anger they've clung to their entire lives; and if they aren't willing to release it, they'll continue to live in pain. You don't have to be right, and you don't have to have all the answers. There is no judgment. Let down your walls, and know that this doesn't have to be done alone.

You just need to uncover the hidden and dark parts of yourself that you may not want to acknowledge, talk about, or bring to the light. You probably like keeping these parts of yourself—rage, anger, and resentment—in the dark and out of view. But if you have a true desire to be connected with your energy source; plant a new Garden that matters; and live a life on your terms full of freedom, creativity, and joy, then you have to accept all aspects of yourself.

Those obstacles in your Life Garden are not going away. That boulder in the corner is going to sit there taking up space and preventing you from planting what you really want until you decide to move it. Those tangled roots beneath the surface aren't going to magically disappear unless you do the work to pull them out. And that wild brush that has overtaken your beautiful rosebushes is not going to leave until you prune it back or rip it out.

Identifying our emotions can be a liberating experience, especially if we've been keeping ourselves down for years—and many times we keep ourselves down for no good reason. I believe that we all have a light inside of us just waiting to burn brightly and illuminate the world. We need to find it, make a clearing for it to grow, and then give it the fuel it needs to thrive.

Pruning, Weeding, and Setting Boundaries

Sometimes, because of the depth of your wounds and years of neglect, you need to work very hard to find your own light. Yet if you want to plant the Seeds of Freedom, then you absolutely must clear away the heavy and dark areas of your Garden. The techniques described in this section should certainly do the trick.

Pruning

Pruning brings energy to what's important in that it clears away the unwanted and gives shape to your Life Garden. You see, as your Garden develops, you may need to remove old blossoms or cut back tree limbs so you don't crowd out growth. Pruning helps you cut out the nonessentials in your life, focusing your energy and giving you the space for what you desire. Sometimes you'll even need to cut off the first blooms in order to have more delicious and bountiful growth throughout the season.

When you first look at the tree that needs pruning, it might seem like an overwhelming job. But upon further inspection, you'll notice that some of the tree is clearly in your way, so it's easy to cut that part out. Then you can take off the obvious deadwood . . . and cut back even more wood to make room for something new to grow the following year. It won't look pretty when you're done, but it's a way to stimulate growth that balances the wildness of nature and the ability to shape what you want in your Garden.

In our lives, we need to cut out things so that we can clear space in our minds. Our lives are much too busy and fast. We forget birthdays, can't coordinate our calendars, or eat dinner with our loved ones with our phones in hand. We're trying to do too much and forget the small, simple things that bring us real joy. It's when we notice the beauty around us—a budding flower, a hummingbird in flight, or a wide-mouthed smile—that we feel nourished. But we're generally so hurried that everything becomes a task, something to check off; in the process, we get caught up in the destination instead of the journey.

When our energy isn't focused, we often miss the connections, beauty, and synchronicities that are on our paths. We miss out on sleep—and then we miss out on the joy of life because we're so tired. We need to take a break from the noise of the everyday so that we can refresh our minds, bodies, and spirits. As a society, we don't place value on being quiet and doing nothing, yet this decompression is absolutely necessary to refuel and rejuvenate for growth. Quietness allows us to stay present and see the subtle vibrations of life so that we can get into the flow of the Universe and trust that everything will work out in its own natural time.

You must create space for yourself, and you can do so by creating space in your calendar. Allowing time to do nothing may seem like a luxury, but it's actually a necessity if you want tap into your creativity and problem-solving abilities. Slow down and engage in heart-centered conversations with a loved one, as this will help you nurture yourself and align your energy for depth of intimacy and connection.

Another (admittedly more radical) thing you can do is to start cancelling things. I'm sure you'll worry that you'll disappoint or offend someone by not attending an event or declining an invitation for a meeting. But what you'll find is that people understand—and some individuals will actually thank you because they didn't want to have the meeting either. Pruning your calendar is similar to pruning a tree. Here's how:

- Get rid of anything that feels as if it's blocking you.
- Cut out all the deadwood, or whatever isn't adding any value to your life.
- Cut out even more so that you have some space for spontaneity, creativity, and just being.

It may feel uncomfortable at first because you're so used to being busy and pleasing everyone around you, but as you prune back your Life Garden, you'll be changing the paradigm about how you live your life. In our world, busyness is a sign of being important or having a purpose. But when you have space on your calendar—and tell others that you have that space—you'll begin to change that notion for us all.

Weeding

If you don't tend to them, weeds will pull energy from your soil and crowd out your roots. Weeds are the people, feelings, and negative behavior patterns that clutter up your life; and they can appear in the form of stuff, activities, or circular and obsessive thinking. It's the gardener's job to clear the weeds out so the important crops can flourish.

Weeds don't go away on their own—they end up dominating whatever space they inhabit. But if you address the problem early, when the weeds first appear, you can pinch them out with two little fingers without causing any pain to your root system. Let them fester, though, and they will strangle out all other growth.

You can clear the weeds in your life by going to your sacred place and asking for assistance, and then listening to the response you get. When you realize that nothing can come into your Life Garden without your invitation, then you receive great freedom from clearing it up. Just pay attention to how you feel, and then you can start to bring harmony to any situation. This is sensitive stuff, so it may take a while to make these changes. You won't really see anything happening at first, but remember that every desire you plant in your Garden will eventually bloom and flourish.

Setting Boundaries

When you have fragile sprouts growing in your vegetable garden, it's important to put up some natural boundaries or even a fence to keep the dog, the neighbors' kids, or the family football game out. Similarly, boundaries can help you figure out what you want to include in your Life Garden, as well as what you'd like to keep out.

This may mean placing restrictions on the people, places, and things you currently allow in your Garden so that you limit the amount of time they spend there. It's important that you only allow in those who are supportive of your growth and what you're cultivating. Time with family and friends is essential to human development—but as your love of self grows, you also need to ensure that you put up the proper fences so that you don't allow others to disrespect you.

Boundaries are an important way of demonstrating that you can take care of yourself, that you don't have to do things not aligned with your higher self, and that you have no tolerance for individuals who don't treat you well. You'll quickly notice when an activity or person leaves you feeling tired or depressed, or if your mood changes from positive to negative after a particular experience. As you monitor the activities in your Garden, you can determine if you want to be a part of those situations in the future.

Transformation and growth in your Garden sometimes means putting up fences to keep unwanted elements from trampling on your fragile dreams. These fences help you manage your energy, and they also provide a gate so that you're aware of who's coming into your Garden and what kinds of things they bring into your life.

As you cultivate the Seeds of Freedom in your own Life Garden, you start to own your power. As you grow the roots of self and nourish them with love, then you have the confidence to state what you need from other people. And you have the courage to open your heart. You can do this by sitting in meditation, nourishing yourself with love, and continuing to work on expanding your viewpoint. When you can open your heart *and* mind, that's when you'll fully realize your power.

You are the co-creator of your Life Garden along with Spirit, and you can create positive outcomes for everyone involved in your life when you set boundaries. These invisible borders set the tone for your Garden and state the intention for what you want to attract into it—the type of people who come in and how they'll treat you, the experiences you want to have, how much abundance you want, how much love you want to share, and how much you want to expand.

When you put up fences, you ask for what you need for the growth of your Garden. Making requests that serve your needs is not being selfish. Rather, this is a self-loving act that is also respectful of other people. When you set your intentions and speak your needs, then all those in your life know what is expected from them, and they can either decide to stay and play in your Garden—or they can leave. Boundaries add clarity to the situation because everyone knows the rules of the game. You love yourself, but you also create the freedom for everyone in the Garden to open his or her heart and feel safe.

Clear Your Field

In the same way that we need tools in the garden to help remove any obstacles, we also require tools to clear our inner fields.

You can clear your field in many ways. It might be a small pebble or weed that can easily be picked up and thrown to the side—or it could be a boulder or entrenched root system for which you need to enlist the help of an expert. Freedom comes from knowing that you always have the ability inside of you, or access to a support system, to handle whatever happens in your Garden.

It's important to learn how to clear your field, so I've outlined some tools you can use to do so in five areas: *environmental, mental, physical, emotional,* and *spiritual.* I use these tools myself to clear up my own Garden, so I can then shape and direct what I want to manifest externally. (Note that some of these tools may have been mentioned in previous sections of the book, but they're repeated here so that you know how to use them when you need to clear out energy from your Life Garden.)

When you know that you have the tools to help you whenever you feel out of control, overly emotional, victimized, or hopeless, then you have the freedom to make changes in your Garden. Go inside, clear your field, and trust the power of your connection to the Universe. The only relationship that matters is the one you have with yourself. Remember that everything in your external environment is just a reflection of what's going on inside of you. Your goal is to clear the obstacles so that your inner *and* outer landscapes match.

1. Environmental Clearing

When I decided to transition my life from Atlanta to Hilton Head, the first thing I had to do was clean up my space. Not only was this part of my spiritual work, but it was also a good way to prepare for the Life Garden that I wanted to create. I decided to go through every single item in my household and "feng shui" my entire life. I threw out clothes that didn't fit. I burned photographs, journals, and cards that had negative memories associated with them. I cleaned old business documents out of my computer, got my financial documents in order, found new doctors to attend to my health-care needs, and repaired everything that was broken in my home.

You can't connect to your spiritual self in the midst of a lot of clutter. Lots of "stuff" doesn't just clog up your physical space—it also clogs you mentally, physically, and emotionally. If you want to clear the clutter from your life, then you need to dig out from the dead energy that no longer serves you.

Everything in life carries a vibration, so there are things that uplift you and add to your growth, and things that drag you down and block your growth. It's time to let go of everything that doesn't have a positive and uplifting effect on your Life Garden. Don't worry if you'll need it someday. If it doesn't fit or bring you joy, or if you don't use it regularly, get rid of it. Clean out your purse, your desk, your basement, your garage, your kitchen, your phone, your computer, and your closets. Wherever you're holding "excess" is where you'll need to start first. If there's no room in your Garden, then nothing new can grow. Let go of what's not serving you.

I must warn you that this project took me more than two years. The process involved countless hours of my time as I sorted through boxes, tried on clothes, and organized my files—but it helped me identify and release so many obstacles that had been holding me back. The space I've now created has given me more freedom and breathing room. It has also released me from some negative patterns that had attached their energy to my hopes, dreams, styles, and behavior. Clearing the clutter from my life freed up space in my mind, and then I was able to more readily connect with the essence of what I really wanted in life . . . and it wasn't *stuff*.

Everything has energy. And although we can't see it, we can definitely sense it. Have you ever been on an elevator when someone else gets on, and you immediately felt fear, darkness, or negativity? Or been in a room with a person whose love of life or happiness radiated and filled up the entire space? If so, then you know how to feel energy.

As I was clearing out my clutter, the most amazing things happened. I'd throw out mementos from a boyfriend, and within days

I'd receive an e-mail from him. I'd throw out presentations from an old job, and before long someone I used to work for would call to say hello. We are all connected energetically, so when I made significant shifts internally, it also rippled out to those in my life.

Think about the flow of life—and note that clutter, dirt, chaos, fighting, and discord all block that flow. Your outer environment is a reflection of your inner life, so if you're carrying a lot of "stuff," then you're holding on to the past. It's a great idea to clear your space of the people, objects, and other elements that don't support your well-being. As you commit to doing things that *do* support your well-being, you'll strengthen your foundation, achieve some clarity, and gain the courage to release and change things in your home. When you clear your space, you balance your life and inspire your soul.

Exercise: Clear the Clutter

Why do we all have so much stuff? Maybe we surround ourselves with possessions because we're not connected to people as much as we used to be. Our individualistic nature makes us believe that we have to have it all. We believe that our possessions are so important that we've sacrificed our connection and reliance on one another.

As I've already mentioned, everything in the environment has a vibration—thoughts, people, possessions, community, food, air, and noise. Go through each room in your house and look at all the stuff in it. As you evaluate each item, consider the following:

- Does it uplift you?
- Does it support your joy?
- Does it hold memories? Are they good or bad?
- Do you own it freely? Are there any attachments or rules surrounding it?

If something doesn't inspire you, bring you joy, or hold positive memories, then let it go. It no longer serves you. Keep in mind that clearing out old energy will allow a newer, higher vibration to come into your life.

More than 200 million people are encumbered by hoarding or simply have too many things. So many of us have gotten caught up in a society of consumption instead of living "light," and we're overwhelmed by the amount of clutter we have in our lives. We just don't need this much stuff!

If you haven't already created an altar, now is the time to make a special place in your home. This is where you'll go when you want to get quiet, pray, or meditate. You can also use this spot as a place to write in your journal, do your gratitude work, or just be.

Creating a special place for you to spend quiet time is a very important part of your journey, and it's about supporting your natural well-being and joy. It demonstrates that you're serious about your commitment, and it's a reminder of how you want to live your life. It's a symbol for what you want to manifest and represents the rooting of your inner world. A special place allows your mind to quiet down, your heart to open, and your spirit to come alive. This is where you can go to get inspired, gain clarity, nurture yourself, root deeply inside, and just sit in silence. It's where you can safely go to feel your emotions, listen for answers, and connect to your higher self.

As you're clearing clutter and creating your altar, it's also important that you're aware of the mood that you're setting in your home. What's your intention for your Life Garden? Think about everything in your residence—as well as all the smells, visual experiences, textures, people, noises, and objects that come from outside your home. This is your sanctuary, and you get to set the tone for it. It's your responsibility to create the energy you want inside your sanctuary, and to manage the energy you allow to come into it. When you care about the energy of your home, you're able to manage your surroundings to support what you want in your Life Garden.

Your environment—your house, your office, your creative space, your car—is a reflection of your inner world. As you connect with that inner world, you may want to make changes in your outer world that reflect how you're feeling or how you want to feel. Make your space delicious so that it nurtures you and you're proud of where you're spending your time. When you do so, you're clearing out anything that doesn't belong in your Life Garden.

2. Mental Clearing

In addition to physical stuff, it's important to also be aware of the mental clutter that's taking up room in your brain. There are many ways to clear this clutter, such as the following:

— **Write it all down.** Keeping a journal is a great way to nourish your emotional self and clear your mental field. A journal is a safe and trusted place for you to purge your feelings, record your thoughts, and confront your fears. You can either put it in a safe place or write stream-of-consciousness style (see the exercise that follows) and burn the pages after you're done. The process of journaling releases the mental clutter from your brain, and releasing that emotional energy is important for future growth and vitality.

Exercise: Extemporaneous Writing

In this exercise, you'll be ridding your mind of all the clutter occupying the space in your brain. You'll be using writing to help empty your mind so that you can access your beliefs and truths:

1. Sit in a quiet spot with a beautiful journal or notebook and a favorite pen.

2. Write free-flowing, without thought, for 15 to 20 minutes. Just keep writing. The purpose is to off-load and upload thoughts. Free-form writing clears the blocks in your subconscious. At first it might just be a "data dump," but as you continue to write day after day, your writing will move into an inspirational and creative space. Do not edit; just write without thought and see what appears.

---

3. Review your writing for ideas and trends. Once you clear the clutter from your mind, you can start to see if there are concepts, ideas, or thoughts that continue to show up in your writing. If you see trends, then it may help you uncover some of the things in your life that need to be cleared out or acted upon.

4. If you have a lot on your mind or there are things you're scared to talk about with anyone, you can do the same exercise with loose sheets of paper. Once you're done with the writing, you can look at it or not. Then burn it or shred it. This is a "mental bath" and will feel like an emotional release or cleansing.

Clearing your mind of the mundane parts of life allows you to access what's in your heart. It's in this space that you're able to feel and process your emotions, let go of things that you're holding on to, or allow creative solutions to float into your consciousness. By doing this exercise daily, you'll be processing all of the nonessential thoughts to access your inner knowing. This exercise deepens your roots as you start to gain access to the clarity of your true self.

— **Meditate.** Committing to a daily meditation practice helps you clear your mind on a regular basis. It doesn't really stop the mental chatter, but it will help you learn how to quiet your mind and connect to your inner knowing. Meditation, prayer, and visualization are good tools to clear your mind so that you can feel a sense of peace and listen to your inner knowing.

— **Give yourself a break.** When your mind is racing to try to find a solution, give yourself a break. You don't have to know all the right answers, anticipate the next move, or have everything figured out. Learn how to go with the flow, relax your mind, and know that the next step will unfold for you in a beautiful way.

— **Say affirmations.** Affirmations allow you to set intentions for your life because they help you use your brain to clear out the unwanted mental chatter and focus only on what you want. By repeating affirmations, mantras, or any other saying that gets you psyched up, you bring awareness to the mental chatter and positively reprogram your brain. Say, "I am free to be me!"

— **Set boundaries.** Setting boundaries with others means that you're taking care of yourself and your Garden first. When you love and care for something, you'll want to protect and cherish it. Note that you need to protect yourself in all of your activities—money, health, work, relationships, and creativity—so that you're making decisions and taking actions that protect your Garden.

3. Physical Clearing

When you have physical pain, that means you're experiencing blocks in the flow of energy or *chi* (pronounced "chee") in your body. Therefore, you need to clear the meridians to help alleviate or eliminate that pain. As I mentioned earlier in the book, moving your body is critical to clearing blocked energy. You can dance, go for a run, or take a swim—whatever feels right for you is what you need to do.

Here are some other helpful ideas:

— **Take a walk in nature.** When asked about a place that made them feel calm, relaxed, and totally free of stress, a great majority of people chose a natural setting such as a beach, the top of a mountain, or a waterfall. This proves that most of us are inspired by nature at our core.

We can feel a connection to all things in the Universe just by going for a walk in nature for 20 minutes each day. The exercise that follows explains this concept in detail.

Exercise: Nature Walk

The purpose of the walk is to connect with nature and clear your mind. It's not about getting your heart rate up, taking the dog out, or saying hello to the neighbors. As you're walking, I'd like you to really connect with nature: pay attention to the trees, the fallen leaves, the caterpillar inching along the grass, and so on.

When you commune with nature on a daily basis in this way, you're able to connect to the divine nature, the place that matters, inside of you. You're in tune with the wisdom of the entire Universe and your higher self.

Here are some things to think about as you walk:

- How do you feel when you really look at and feel nature?
- What inspires you the most?
- Do you see the mystery and magic that surrounds you?
- How does your mood change when you're outside, breathing fresh air?
- What do you hear when you listen to nature?
- Where do you see your God when you go out into nature?

— **Act it out.** You can physically act out your emotions and blocks. You can create and then perform a one-person play, dance it out, or visualize it in your mind. Processing your emotions is a very powerful way to clear your physical field.

— **Try alternative healing practices.** Make an appointment with a healer who specializes in one of the many alternative healing practices out there: acupuncture, chiropractic care, massage, Reiki, reflexology, energy medicine, or some other form that interests you. Many times your body just needs to come back into its wholeness by clearing blocked energy, and these types of treatments can help do so by stimulating your physical energy.

— **Focus on the breath.** Focusing on your breath automatically quiets your mind, brings vitality to your physical body, and returns your attention to the present. Breathing is something that you can do anywhere and anytime without anyone knowing. Just breathe and you immediately clear some energy from your field. Take a deep breath now. Inhale . . . exhale. Feel better?

— **Do a cleanse.** There are several ways to cleanse your body. Whether you choose to fast, try a juice or raw diet, or slough the dead skin cells off your body by dry brushing, cleansing is a great way to clear your body of unwanted energy, wake up the system, and bring clarity and vitality to your life. I try to do a raw-food cleanse with the change of the seasons, but you can find out what works for you and what makes you feel physically clear.

4. Emotional Clearing

When you have emotional energy clogged in your field, you may not have anything physically wrong with you, but you probably do feel heavy or blocked. When you feel this way, you can easily do one of the following things to help clear your emotional energy:

— **Drink water.** When you drink a glass of water, it immediately calms down your nervous system. Therefore, this is the easiest, most portable way to reduce anxiety, connect with your emotions, and clear your emotional field.

— **Take a sea-salt bath.** I mentioned this in previous chapters, but taking a bath with a handful of sea salt for 20 minutes is an extremely effective way to clear your emotional field. The salt actually draws energy from your field, stripping any unwanted or negative energy, leaving you clear to connect to yourself and your energy source.

This is a good way to clear your stress and help relax your nervous system. If you only do one thing from this book, I urge you to spend time soaking in a bath.

— **Have a temper tantrum.** A controlled tantrum—whether it's by screaming into a pillow or towel or kicking your feet and banging your hands—is a good way to clear unwanted emotional energy trapped in your body. It may seem childish, but if you're really upset about something that doesn't seem to make sense, then you've triggered something in your emotional body. And a great way to spend some time honoring that feeling is by having a temper tantrum!

— **Light your way.** You can clear your emotional field by visualizing that you're standing under a clear white light. Imagine that this light is filling your entire body with loving energy. This light not only clears your emotional body, but it also protects you and raises up your vibration as well. Like flipping on a switch in an unlit room, filling your body with light energy instantly clears any darkness.

— **Sing a song.** If you remember the Carpenters or *Sesame Street,* you may remember the hit tune "Sing." It's good advice, since singing or toning helps you connect to a universal and harmonious vibration. Singing clears your emotional field because you connect to the vibration of the Universe, and it fills you with a feeling of well-being and happiness. Belt it out in the shower or the car, or just softly sing something wherever you are, to clear away any negative or heavy feelings that you may have.

5. Spiritual Clearing

If you're not in the flow of life or tapped into the power of the Universe, it might be time for some spiritual cleansing. You could be blocked in this area if you're holding resentment toward others, trying to control everything, or not allowing your creativity to flow. When you feel this way, there are several things you can do to clear your spiritual field:

— **Forgive yourself and others.** Forgiveness of yourself is critical to clearing your field. When you let go of past hurts and mistakes and forgive yourself and others, then you clear the way for vitality and love. Forgive and acknowledge all experiences, no matter how terrible they may seem, as a gift that you've received. This simple act frees you from any past pain, trauma, resentment, or shame so that you can move forward in the future. You can't plant new things until you've removed the old, so once you do so, you'll immediately feel lighter. When you forgive, you'll feel a sense of peace and calm. It's a powerful way to clear your spiritual energy.

— **Surrender to the Universe.** If you have a sincere desire to connect with your spiritual being and really know all dimensions of yourself, then you'll be clearing the way for open communication. The important issue here is sincerity. When you take an action with the intention of getting something, it won't work—but when you genuinely want to live a life aligned with the power of the Universe, you clear the way for miracles, spiritual assistance, and magic.

— **Claim your power and send back unwanted energy.** It's quite possible that you're holding on to energy that doesn't belong to you. You might be shouldering the burden of a past relationship or job, or maybe you gave away your power in a business relationship. Whatever it is, you can clear your field by sending the energy you're holding back to the other person so that he or she can be whole—and then you can claim your energy back so that you can come into *your* wholeness. This method is best done at your altar or special place, as it is a sacred energy of the spiritual realm. Sending back unwanted energy and then claiming what you've given away helps you clear your spiritual field so that you can release attachment and own your power.

— **Express appreciation.** Appreciate all the good in your life and thank the Universe for all of your blessings, no matter how big or small. Gratitude links your mind, body, and soul together in harmony and raises your vibration. Appreciation clears the way for more things to come into your life. Appreciate, appreciate, and appreciate again! We all have so many blessings when we just take the time to see them.

— **Do something creative.** You may want to dance, compose a piece of music, or paint a picture to clear your energy field. When you allow your emotions to flow through you by creating, you're experiencing the emotions as you create. It's a great way to clear your spiritual energy and tap into something greater than yourself for inspiration. You might also be pleasantly surprised by your ability to express yourself creatively.

Clear the Way for Assistance

If you've been working on your Life Garden, you have made a very important commitment to yourself and have started to cultivate a life that really does matter. As you build your foundation and start to work with your energy, though, you may find that you come to a point when you are stuck and can't go any farther. It's at these times when you need to solicit the help of a guide so that you can benefit from that person's expertise.

We all need help when we're seeking greatness—an athlete hires a coach, a climber enlists the aid of a Sherpa, an apprentice studies with a master. Every one of us needs assistance from time to time to break through to the next level. This is not a sign of weakness, but rather of strength. It takes courage to know when to ask for help.

You might not know how to handle the energy that wants to move through you, or you'll need someone to aid you in accessing that energy so you can release it. Whatever the reason, you're going to need some support. In the same way that a dentist can alleviate your toothache, a holistic facilitator can release any stuck energy in your body. This person can also help guide you through difficult terrain and onto a smoother path.

It's a good bet that as soon as you put the request out to the Universe, you'll magically see an advertisement, a friend will send you an e-mail, or you'll be talking to someone who will bring up the perfect practitioner for this type of work. Finding a professional who can help you release energy is a very personal experience, so you're going to have to use your own judgment to find the right individual for you. When the student is ready, the teacher always appears.

When I was ready to release control and try something different, a friend recommended Summer, my holistic practitioner, to me. I'm so grateful that she's come into my life to guide me on my journey, since I couldn't have transformed my life to the extent I have without her guidance and spiritual assistance. I still had to do the inner work myself, but she was there to support me along the way, giving me encouragement and assistance when I needed it.

Our emotions are like magnets that draw people, places, and events to us. When we are detached from our emotions and allow them to course through us, then we can be light and go with the flow . . . and we're able to grow what we want in our Life Garden.

As we get more spiritually connected to ourselves and our source energy, we're able to see life from a place of multidimensionality. We can then clear the communication channel to listen to our emotions, feelings, intuition, and gut reactions so that we can live in alignment with our purpose and our higher selves.

You've learned that when you clear your own field internally, you shift what happens externally. You now know that the power of spirit or love can dissolve all fear, hate, and sickness. And what you're left with is a freedom that you will always have peace, no matter what is happening in your world.

In this chapter, you learned how to plant the seed of clearing, and you discovered the tools that you can use to go within and find your peace and find your freedom. In the next chapter, you'll be planting the last seed in your Life Garden—the seed of renewal.

Digging Deeper: The Elephant in the Garden

If you want to dig deeper and clear out those boulders in your garden, then you can:

1. Ask for help. Ask your loved ones what they see in your Garden. This may be a difficult exercise, but do ask three to five close friends, colleagues, or family members to answer these two questions: (1) "Name five things that you think are my special talents, gifts, and contributions to the world"; and (2) "Name five things that you think are blocking my success."

Note that it's easier for other people to see our gifts and our obstacles because they have an objective view. Think of the alcoholic who finally admits that he has a problem, which everyone in his life already knew—they were just waiting for him to figure it out and talk about that "elephant in the room." If you're open to asking for help, your friends and family can help you spot your own elephant.

2. Read *The Shadow Effect: Illuminating the Hidden Power of Your True Self*. This book by Deepak Chopra, Debbie Ford, and Marianne Williamson is a deep exploration of the things you try to hide within yourself, your shadow. It will aid you in identifying those boulders in your life that you may not want to uncover, and it will also help you understand why it's important to clear them from your Life Garden.

3. Clear out one thing in your life. Clean out your desk at work, your purse, your car, the hall closet, the garage, or your medicine cabinet. When you clean out just one thing that is weighing you down or clogging up your energy, then you're taking a step in the right direction to clear out your Garden. Digging deeper is difficult, so start small—do one thing, and see what happens. As the old metaphor goes, the only way to eat an elephant is one bite at a time.

CHAPTER NINE

RENEWAL

"Happiness is the meaning and the purpose of life,
the whole aim and end of human existence."

— A R I S T O T L E

When First Lady Michelle Obama took up residence at 1600 Penn-sylvania Avenue, one of the first things she did was plant a garden, which was the first one at the White House since Eleanor Roosevelt's victory garden in World War II. Mrs. Obama wanted to provide fresh produce for her family, as well as for formal dinners; so she decided to plant collard greens, kale, arugula, and berries. She is also using the garden as a way to educate children about healthy, locally grown fruits and vegetables.

There are more than one million community gardens in the United States. The interest in urban garden renewal and using land to share the duties and bounties of a garden continues to grow, particularly as the trend toward healthier eating continues to rise—along with concerns that our food is contaminated or carrying disease, geneti-cally modified or chemically laden products are invading our stores, and mass-produced fruits and vegetables are adversely impacting our planet.

Such increased interest is a very good thing, since there are a lot of lessons that can be learned by connecting to the earth through a garden. Gardening can be a humbling experience, but it's also a great way to learn about the rebirth of life.

Many communities today are struggling, and not just economically; they're having a very difficult time remaining positive in such dire times. But when folks get together and plant a garden, there's a sense of optimism. There's not only the hope that people will develop more healthy eating habits, but that they will be renewed emotionally and spiritually as well. Gardens teach us that there is always hope: What looks like a pile of garbage is actually the food for next year's crops. What looks like a patch of plain dirt is actually fertile ground packed with potential. What looks like a dead tree is actually just taking a rest during the long winter months so that it can be renewed in the spring. We discover that any seemingly negative situation can be turned into something positive for all parties involved.

Working with the Seasons and Cycles of Nature

In a garden, stuff dies. Annuals die back every year, but even perennials can suddenly experience a shift and wither away, leaving us scratching our heads and wondering why. That's just the way it is in a garden. Yet it affords us the opportunity to become better gardeners, and teaches us how to put even death to good use.

Whenever plant matter dies, we're able to pull it out of the garden, put it to the side in a composting pile, and give it time to transform. This dead plant material that we remove in the fall becomes the fertilizer that helps us next spring. It's an ever-present ritual of renewal.

We can perform the same ritual in our Life Gardens. The brief activities or relationships we planted that didn't quite take, the career paths we pursued but then realized weren't right for us, the trials and errors, the failures and successes—they all die back at some point.

When they do, we may set them aside for a time, but they won't really be gone. Instead, they'll be transforming themselves into fuel for the coming harvest.

Our experiments are never mistakes, even if they do turn out to be disastrous. Our "mistakes" fuel our future growth and expansion. As I said in the Introduction, we don't learn by listening to others, taking seminars, or reading lots of books. We learn through experience. So we need to go out and make mistakes and gain that experience. In the process, we'll grow and change in ways we never could have imagined.

All parts of a garden are important, even those that are no longer alive. Once they've hit the compost pile, they begin the miraculous process of renewal that death ushers in. This ultimately transforms the inanimate into the animate, the failed into a new possibility for success, and even death itself into life. The same is true in our Life Gardens. We're using our experiences to grow, to push us forward to achieve what we really want, and to transform our lives into a vision of vibrancy.

It's important to remember that there's a season for everything in our lives, and when we learn to understand each season, then we can act accordingly. When we're in harmony with the Universe, we're able to work with the processes of nature instead of trying to force something to grow when it's time to lie fallow, for instance. In a garden, there's a season for planting, a season for growth, a season for harvest, and a season for rest and renewal.

In order to renew our Life Gardens, we have to remember that we can't be producing all the time. Productivity and focus must shift and rotate as the seasons of our lives change. And sometimes we have to accept the fact that the season demands that we sit and do nothing until conditions have improved. When we're aware of this, we don't have to try so hard to make something grow that simply won't. We can take a sabbatical while our Gardens rest.

When I'm advising clients who have quit or lost their jobs, I tell them to wait a little while before looking for employment. I tell them to take a few weeks off and renew themselves by taking a vacation, getting in shape, and having fun. Then when they've replenished themselves, we begin to talk about how to address their work situation.

The same is true if you've just gone through a breakup. If you've been in a relationship for a long time and it ends, it's dangerous to jump right into another one. This section of your Life Garden needs time to heal and restore itself on its own. If you're hopping from one relationship to another, then you never give your emotional system time to heal. You never get to know yourself *by yourself.* Since you haven't experienced that part of yourself, you won't be totally whole when you're in your next relationship. You'll always be dependent on another person to make you feel good.

Let yourself go fallow. Don't rush into a demanding job or a new relationship. Spend time on yourself. Allow yourself to breathe . . . and to transform.

You may be uncomfortable because you're in between things right now—in between jobs, relationships, or phases of life, perhaps—and you feel lonely and lost. Yet I visualize such a time as a hallway: At one end of the hall is the life you've left behind, and you just haven't made it to the other end yet. It's an unknown place, but you can see a light down there and are drawn to keep moving toward it, even though it's scary and new. This in-between time is critical to your self-development. When you can be comfortable in a long hallway all alone—without a partner, without a title, without a job—then you'll really get to know yourself.

As you transition, you simply need to remember that there is nothing wrong. In fact, everything is just right. And as long as you accept that even the dead of winter plays its role in nature, and have faith that spring will come again, you can relax with the flow of your growth and enjoy every season in your Garden, without fear.

It's also important to rotate your crops every season, which stimulates renewal. In a physical garden, if you try to grow tomatoes in the same patch every year, you're going to get pests, disease, and poor production. Renewal means shaking things up, trying out new territories and environments, and giving your soil the diversity it needs to stay healthy and vital. In the process, you'll be able to follow the direction of your alignment and be open to possibilities.

Shaking things up can be fun. It can be playful. It can make life more interesting and certainly gives you a fresh perspective. So when you're in between growing seasons, take your attention off of your Life Garden for a little while and go have some fun. Fun changes the energy, and you learn what brings you joy and what doesn't. The things you don't like just get tossed into the compost pile.

In a crowded room, people will know I'm there because of my laugh. Laughing is actually one of my most favorite activities in the world, and anyone who can make me laugh is a friend for life. Laughter is a vibration of joy that reverberates throughout space—and it's infectious, too. Of course, I'll laugh alone if I see something funny, but it's best when shared with others. Fun is essential in my Life Garden, and I enjoy having individuals around me who feel the same way. Laughter is one of the ways that I renew myself and stay light and joyful, even when I'm alone in the hallway.

Fun, play, and laughter give you freedom and renew your spirit. Even Leonardo da Vinci made play a regular practice, and Albert Einstein once said that he wished he'd played more. Play allows for creativity, innovation, and new ideas to pop into your consciousness. It's an important part of being a full person and living a life that matters, so that your soil is rich and fertile when it comes time to plant again.

Children certainly don't have a problem with this: They sing, laugh, and make up games all day long. They jump in puddles with pure exhilaration, make jewelry for their friends with unconditional love, and draw pictures of their surroundings with intense vibrancy. They aren't afraid of coloring outside the lines (unless we teach them not to). We adults should be the same way.

Learning new things means making mistakes, being courageous, and losing control. We're continually evolving, so one creation in our lives won't define us forever. We are born to create, and our creativity is a life-giving process. We won't be happy until we align with the stream of connection and creative expression, experience the freedom to be our best selves, and find our joy and share it with the world!

It's really important that you continue to inject some fun into everything you do in your Life Garden. Sometimes working in your Garden might seem pointless, as if you're doing a lot and not getting a lot out of it. That's when you need to take a break and just let go. Have a dance party in your living room, go see a funny movie, or take the kids outside for a game of hide-and-seek. Whatever you do, look for the lighter side of the situation. Once you're able to take the heaviness out of your life or a specific situation, then it's much easier to think clearly and know that whatever you're facing will work out just fine.

You can also use play and fun to help you shed your fears, explore new ways of being, or move through new experiences. As you create your Life Garden, you'll be keeping the atmosphere joyful and positive for all involved.

We renew our lives by having fun, keeping our hearts open, and anticipating good things. When we're able to interject fun and joy in our lives, then we're returning to our natural state. We're able to transform all experiences—good, bad, or boring—into the fuel for our future. We're able to see the possibilities in our life and know that if we can imagine it, it can come true. And we wait with anticipation for all the good things to come, like the buds on a tree in the springtime; we are in constant renewal no matter where we are right now.

Renew Your Dreams and Possibilities

When I started planning my Life Garden, I desperately wanted a husband and children. I felt insignificant and incomplete without a family, so I did everything I could to plant its seeds in my Garden: I quit my job, threw myself into trying to find the perfect partner, and then spent a great deal of time in a significant relationship. I investigated having a child on my own, and then I finally started to break down my own beliefs of what "family" has to look like.

As I got older, I discovered that the chances of conceiving a child on my own were more difficult. My Western doctors didn't give me much hope because of my age—or, more shockingly, because I wasn't married. One of my doctors actually told me that I should have a husband before I even thought about having a baby (as you may imagine, I stopped going to her immediately). I also found out that my insurance wouldn't cover me if I did get pregnant because I wasn't married or on a family plan. So I sought out alternative methods of healing to understand my fertility options, and I made sure to be around those individuals who were accepting of my current situation as a single woman wanting to bear a son or daughter.

It was this desperate search to uncover my ability to have a child, as well as to find the right people who could help me, that assisted me in questioning my beliefs deep in my soul and uncover my truth. The surprise for me was when I woke up one day and realized that I had stopped thinking about a husband and baby and had started getting excited about other things that were blossoming in my life—writing a book, starting a new business, and continuing my own transformational work. When I looked around my Garden at this point and thought about what I really wanted to grow, having a child wasn't so important anymore. Although modern medicine had allowed for the possibility, my old dream had died and a new one had taken its place.

As we plant our Life Gardens, we need to keep in mind that they'll always be growing and changing, so we'll need to tend to their care and renew our soil throughout our lives. This includes our dreams and possibilities—we must invent and reinvent our financial security, our relationships with friends, our vocation, our health and wellness, and our connection to the spirit world. These Gardens need to be continually rotated, replenished, and recycled. We have to learn to accept that dreams do sometimes die, but they'll be reborn as new possibilities. This acceptance will allow us to live happily with the changes in our lives and be at peace in the knowledge that all is well in our Gardens, as long as there is growth.

The Seeds of Freedom are not something we plant once and then forget about. If we want to be free and cultivate a life that matters, then we must regularly renew and refine our lives to create what makes us happy. If we're growing, then we're adapting and morphing in new ways based on what we've learned about ourselves and our

Ashford Chancelor's Story

My colleague Ashford Chancelor has a passion for purpose. As vice president of finance at The Wilderness Society, he's on a mission to grow and develop a leading nonprofit organization in conservation and sustainability. But he hasn't always been so engaged in the world beyond his own.

Ashford grew up in Texas in a conservative, traditional home. After graduating from Texas Tech University, he went to work for a top accounting firm, where he learned the basics of business and finance. He was then recruited by a small but rapidly growing investment company—and, although the work was exhausting, he was energized by the dynamics of the business. After the company was sold, he seized the opportunity to reassess the next phase of his life and career.

While completing his MBA at Southern Methodist University, my colleague was asked to do some work with the Young Presidents' Organization (YPO), a nonprofit membership organization of young business leaders throughout the country. Ashford realized that there was little this group of leaders couldn't accomplish with their combined resources and connections; it was a powerful group indeed. He wondered how he could harness these resources for greater missions to improve the world. He stayed with YPO after he finished his MBA, unaware that he would also begin a spiritual transformation that would change his life.

After enduring a string of personal tragedies, Ashford embarked on a quest to find greater meaning in his life. He calls this period his "dark night of the soul," much like that described by Saint John of the Cross in his epic poem, "La noche oscura del alma." It was a time of isolation and grief for Ashford, yet it ultimately led to unimaginable growth and transformation.

Ashford studied world religions and even metaphysics, reading and learning voraciously in his search for relief and enlightenment. But every path he explored led him back to God, and to a calling to seek a higher and greater purpose for his life beyond his own self-interests. Every aspect of his life—physical, mental, and spiritual—became so profoundly changed that on his 50th birthday, he legally changed his name from his birth name, which he no longer wants to acknowledge, to Ashford Chancelor (a name that came to him from God) to mark his rebirth and renewal.

Today Ashford dedicates his time to causes that seek to improve society and the world. He knows innately that this is his purpose, but he admits he hasn't "arrived" yet; he continues to renew himself, seek guidance, and embrace greater empowerment every day. He begins and ends his days in prayer and tries to live each moment in a conscious and authentic way. When I asked him what a life of freedom means to him, he said, "Freedom can mean the ability to do things that bring joy to your heart. So, using that perspective, to me freedom means having the unfettered ability to bring joy, to be uplifting, and to spread love to everyone I can."

environment, along with what we're interested in during that particular season of our lives.

The process is always teaching you something—like a gardener, you get smarter each year, you try out new things, your skills develop, and your tastes change. You realize that it's not the best idea to plant the same thing year after year. Change is good. Experience is good.

You may remember that earlier in the book, I talked about the importance of creating, and then writing down, a vision for your life. I've transformed so much since I first started my Garden that I decided to come up with a new vision for myself, one that is more in alignment with my current life—that is, what I want to create and what matters to me now. Here's the condensed version of what I wrote:

I see each moment of each day as the potential for a new beginning. I see the divinity of Spirit in all living things, and I live my life in alignment with my higher self. I choose love, peace, truth, vitality, clarity, courage, and to see life full of unlimited possibilities.

I see myself enjoying and exercising my freedom every day. I am here to be of service by living authentically in all areas of my life. I live my life in alignment with my spiritual connection and follow the guidance and inspiration I receive. I see myself making a difference in the lives of many individuals worldwide—and my book, <u>Seeds of Freedom: Cultivating a Life That Matters,</u> serves as a message of hope for those who want to live a more authentic life.

I am healthy and fit and maintain such wellness by making time for exercise, meditation, and contemplation on a daily basis. I also eat fresh and nutritious meals wherever I am; and I make time for sleep, rest, hot baths, and just being. I enjoy my time in Hilton Head with my family at the beach, sailing, playing tennis, riding bikes, and just relaxing in my garden.

My relationships with my partner, family, and friends are easy and loving. We make time for one another and enjoy each other's company. I enjoy being with these people, and everyone in my life gets along well. I am in a relationship with an incredibly talented, healthy, fun, and loving man who is also aligned with connection—and we are joyfully co-creating our Life Gardens together.

I am engaging with people from around the world as I travel in an RV with my partner, my parents, friends, and my dogs. I see myself treating all these new individuals that I meet with kindness, love, and respect. I travel often and spend very little time in an office or sitting in front of a computer. I enjoy speaking to large groups of people, consulting with individuals and corporations, writing books, hosting a radio and TV show, organizing conferences, and other creative outlets that come out of the work I'm doing that raises consciousness in the world.

I see myself setting up my business in a way that I can set my own schedule, even when I'm on the road in the RV. My business is growing organically by going with the flow and exploring the possibilities that naturally unfolds for me. I see myself being authentic, transparent, and collaborative with the people that I engage with on a professional level. I see myself doing work that has a lot of variety and is creative and fun. My team is an amazing group of highly connected, creative, and talented individuals who are passionate about the work we're doing and the impact we can make on the world.

I don't worry about money; it flows easily and abundantly through a variety of channels. I have financial security in my life with a strong bank account; along with multiple homes in Atlanta, Hilton Head Island, and somewhere on the West Coast. I enjoy selecting the interior designs of these homes and am able to choose natural, organic, and handcrafted items that fill me with inspiration and joy. I have a sense of freedom about my finances and am amazed by what money allows me to do in my life: assist people in living their dreams, build retreat centers, empower women around the world, plant gardens to help people connect with the earth and eat healthy and nutritious food, and transform the way we do business.

I see my business flourishing as I help businesses tap into the new human technologies of intuition, empathy, compassion, and wisdom using heart-centered leadership. I see myself helping businesses redefine success so people don't have to sacrifice their health and well-being, their relationships, and their passions and freedoms in order to make money to live. I see myself helping people transform their own lives which ultimately transforms the world.

My life is a lot of fun and full of unexpected surprises and magic, and my schedule allows for spontaneity. My heart is open, and my radiance and love shine through to everyone I meet. I take time to travel for pleasure, enjoy creative pursuits, and spend time in my garden . . . just being totally present in the moment. I am perfect just as I am. I know that what we do to cultivate our own Life Gardens matters, and I am living my life according to my alignment and connection to God-consciousness. My life is delicious. My life is exceptional. My life is flourishing, and I am living a life of freedom.

We all have the ability to choose how we want to feel and what we want to create in our lives. When we're aware of this, we're connected to what's going on in all dimensions of our existence and can then become the deliberate creators of our Life Gardens through our thoughts and actions. As we fully connect to ourselves through our connection to our energy source, we're able to heal any pain; easily give and receive the love, joy, and peace that we desire; and experience freedom. Cultivating our spiritual lives allows our everyday lives to expand so that we can be thoroughly renewed.

Life is about reaching for new possibilities, figuring out what we want to do, and then letting the Universe show us the unfolding of that desire. When we plant the Seeds of Freedom in our Gardens, we're then free to choose from an infinite number of possibilities life makes available to us. We're not confined by any external forces when we're connected to our energy source.

If we only desire that which we can conceive, then nothing will ever change. When we only observe what is and make decisions from that standpoint, then we will continue to cut off the natural growing cycle. We need to trust the Universe and know that it is made up of cycles and seasons and possibilities and potential. It's in this place of belief that the creations in our Life Garden are unlimited. *Anything is possible.*

Anticipate Your Possibilities

In one of my favorite childhood books, there's a part that I love that reads: "'Well,' said Pooh, 'what I like best—' and then he had to stop and think. Because although Eating Honey *was* a very good thing to do, there was a moment just before you began to eat it which was better than when you were, but he didn't know what it was called." That feeling is called *anticipation.*

When we're in a state of anticipation, we are expectant, full of hope, and excited—it's a state of joy and a process of renewal. When we anticipate what's growing in our Life Gardens, then not only are we content where we are in the present moment, but we're excited about what's coming, too. We're appreciative of everything that we have right now . . . even if it only looks like a tray of dirt. We don't see lack, and we enjoy the moment regardless of the circumstances. But we also know that we have great plans for our Gardens and are eagerly looking forward to what's to come.

Anticipation is what drives us forward to create and expand. Then we can both enjoy our day-to-day lives and be excited by what's on the horizon. It's similar to when women find out that they're pregnant: they don't stop living, but they *do* start preparing—physically, mentally, and emotionally—for the way things will change in the future. We typically have nine months to prepare for a new addition to the family, and there is great anticipation about the arrival of that baby. The same is true in business. Mergers, new product launches, or system implementations often take years to put in place—and project leaders and teams enjoy the hard work, the problem solving, and the anticipation of the "big day." It's never solely about the end result; the anticipation and excitement building up to it are often just as important.

You may feel as if you want what you want right now, but there's a buffer of time between what you say you desire and its appearing in your life. This anticipation period is 99 percent of the creation, so have fun with that part as well. It's not about getting what you want—the journey is about the anticipation and then the getting. The fun is in the experience of creating what you would like and then allowing the surprises, magic, and enthusiasm to fill your Life Garden as you co-create with your energy source.

Once you trust that you're creating your Life Garden in partnership with the Universe, then you can start to see unlimited possibilities for creation. Creative expression is really the only way to find your purpose and fulfillment in the world. It's the way to tap into your gifts and discover what fills you with enthusiasm. Once you start creating, you'll move forward on your path—and, in the process, you may just end up facing your darkest fears and your most sublime moments.

If you're not manifesting what you want in your Garden, you may want to start appreciating everything in your life right now—the roof over your head, the food on your table, the relationships you share with your family and friends, and the health you enjoy. It's also a good idea to stay patient and calm as you wait for the manifestation, reminding yourself that there is a perfect timing to how everything unfolds.

A garden is made up of a series of small steps, such as seeds that we plant and overgrowth we need to prune. As we create and do the work, we'll always want more: We'll want to try new things. We'll want to plant new varieties. We'll want to make it bigger. We do so because it feels good to expand. I think it's exciting to move beyond where we thought we could.

When you're totally aligned with your Life Garden—when you're completely in tune with your deepest desires and purpose in the world, you've cleared out all the blocks and negative thinking, and you've filled yourself with gratitude—then your creations flow easily from you with joy and enthusiasm and a constant process of renewal. It's a delicious process, which you'll experience in all aspects of your existence. This is what pure freedom feels like: it's exhilarating. Your creative expression and expansion in your Life Garden is the purpose of life; it's what really matters.

It's Time to Redefine Success

Renewal is about redefining success as conditions in our Gardens change. We don't have to maintain our financial status, physical appearance, professional station, marital status, or creative expression as one linear prescription throughout our lifetimes. When we're in sync with the seasons of life—when we realize our own value because we're connected to our higher, spiritual selves—then we know that we can enjoy our triumphs, but they don't define us.

What is your definition of success? Is it based on internal or external factors? Know that when you base your success criteria on things outside of you, it's like planting a garden on a flatbed truck: it might seem safe and secure when the truck is parked in your driveway, but as soon as someone else gets behind the wheel, goes too fast, or gets in an accident, then your beautiful creation crumbles in front of you. It may seem like a silly metaphor, but this is what happens when the stock market crashes; you get bad news at the doctor's office; you find out the executives at your trusted workplace have been deceiving you; your relationship ends; or you're forced to change your creations because of demands from "higher-ups," politicians, or other authority figures exerting their power and control.

But when your definition of success is based on what matters to you internally, then you're the only one who gets to decide what's best for you, and what stays and what goes. You're not trying to please anyone outside of yourself—you know that everyone is growing his or her Life Garden at different phases. You're in alignment with your own connection, and you maintain an inner sense of security at all times.

You understand that the experiences you've endured, no matter how terrible, have given you the fuel you needed to create your ideal Garden. You wouldn't be the person you are today without these experiences. You have an unwavering sense of freedom to express yourself, to see possibilities, and to try something new. You are aligned with your spiritual self and are authentic. You go with the flow of life and act on inspiration and your trusted intuition. That's your definition of success.

You also know that you can only win if *everyone* wins. You know that the old way of working based on competition, win-lose, and greed doesn't fly in the Garden. Imagine if society actually defined success based on the integrity and alignment of a person instead of external measures. What if businesses were measured on the amount of good they did instead of on the bottom line?

We can thrive in these complex times if we are open to seeking a new way of being, a new way of thinking, a new definition of success that values the inner world as much as the outer world.

Exercise: Redefining Success

It's time to redefine your definition of success, to give yourself permission to focus on what you want and renew your sense of freedom in life. Remember, you're perfect just being you, you're a spiritual being living a physical experience, and the purpose of your life is your creative expression.

Based on what you've learned in this book so far, let's do an exercise to help you redefine success. In your journal or notebook, answer the following questions:

- What represents success for you?
- How do you measure success?
- Is there an external source that defines, or has power over, your success?
- Does this definition of success match what you desire in your Life Garden?
- Is there anything in this definition that you could put in the compost pile? If so, what is it?
- Metaphorically, what season are you right now: winter, spring, summer, or fall?
- Are any of your dreams able to grow in this season?
- Is it time to transplant or rotate any crops in your Garden? If so, what needs to be transplanted or rotated?

Based on your answers (and what you've learned in this book), do you think you need to redefine your definition of success for yourself? Do you need to be kinder, gentler, and more patient? Do you need to focus on planting something different, since no matter how hard you try, you'll never get a tomato to grow in the dead of winter? End the exercise by writing down your new definition of success.

Every day as I tend to the plants in my garden, I find myself enjoying the process and acknowledging how I feel at that moment. When I remember to pause and appreciate that twinkling moment of pleasure, I know that I've done my work right.

Success is as simple as this, an ability to enjoy the present at every moment. I don't have to "do" anything or work hard—I just have to keep appreciating and acknowledge the slivers of joy in the moment. And when I can remember how I feel when I'm in the garden, then I have a set point for how I want to feel as I deal with customer-service agents, traffic, and lines at the grocery store.

If you can just focus on the good feeling that you have in your Life Garden, then you can catch the flow of this feeling anytime you want. You can train yourself to carry this feeling with you wherever you are in the world—be it at the office, on a blind date, or in bed at night.

No matter where you are, you can feel the freedom from your current circumstances and the anticipation of achieving what you dream of growing in each area of your Garden: the money you desire, the body weight you choose, the meaningful job you're searching for, and the relationships you crave are all there in that feeling of exhilaration in the moment.

If you allow the appreciation of each moment to constantly renew your Life Garden, then you'll be amazed by the inspiration that flows into your being. Whenever you align with your source, you'll have the Universe on your side—you'll have the creative energy to paint the picture, make the business deal, or start a new job. You'll be divinely inspired to help create your flourishing Life Garden.

Exercise: 30 Days of Renewal

You can't expect more good without appreciation for what you already have, so don't take things for granted. As you appreciate what you have, then it allows your energy to handle bigger things—you'll be able to expand and create even more in the world. Appreciation allows you to renew. However, if you focus on the deficiencies in your life and aren't grateful for what you already have, then the powers of the Universe won't trust you with more, and you'll continue to live in that lack-consciousness.

For one month, I'd like you to carve out time each day to do the following:

1. Turn off all the noise in your life—be it your TV, phone, computer, radio, or iPod. You're also going to have to clear your schedule of dates or obligations with other people whenever possible, asking everyone for understanding and support.

2. Spend time outside to light the flame of your desires. In your journal, write down all the beautiful and intricate details that you see there (or in nature around you, if you don't have a garden). Pay attention to a leaf and describe its color, texture, shape, and smell. Tune in to the amazing sights, sounds, and fragrances that make you happy or stir your soul. Write as much as you can, and when you stop writing, just sit and *be.* When you appreciate, you can be totally present in the moment. You'll look for positive aspects instead of zeroing in on what's wrong; you'll only see good and beauty. In that moment, all will truly be well in the world.

3. One of the most powerful tools to shift your vibration is gratitude. So each night before you go to bed, celebrate your gifts and appreciate all that is good in your life—be sure to only focus on the positive. When you do this right before sleep, it will fill you with the deliciousness of life and help you recognize how much joy is all around you, each and every day.

When the month is over, pay attention to all the ways in which your life has changed. I'm sure you'll be in for a very pleasant surprise!

Renew Your Freedom

After months of clearing the clutter from my home in Atlanta, I put it on the market and continued to sort, clean, clear, and purge for another two years. The house didn't sell, but I was able to lease it and move full-time to Hilton Head Island. The move gave me the freedom that I desired, financially, professionally, creatively, and energetically. When I left that big house—the symbol of my old world of security, control, and conformity—it was as if a weight had been lifted off my body. I felt as if I were finally released from that previous life and could start anew.

Living at the beach is incredible in so many ways. I have a deep connection to the ocean and spend most mornings taking a walk to soak in the salty air and clear my mind. What I love about the beach is that there is constant renewal. No matter what has happened the day before, the tides will wash it away and leave the coastline fresh again. When I take my morning walks, my footprints are the first and only ones there in the sand. It's a very soulful experience to see the sunrise with the vast ocean and unblemished beach in front of me. It reminds me that the day is full of possibilities, it doesn't matter what happened yesterday, and I don't have to worry about tomorrow. I just have to be totally immersed in this moment.

Yet the garden was where I first learned to renew my spirit. I opened my mind, healed my heart, and connected with my higher self. It's where I rediscovered my enthusiasm for life. Initially, it took courage to plant the garden—I had no idea what I was doing or that it was going to change my life. Nevertheless, I ended up finding my truth and joy, along with creativity I didn't even know I had.

Although the garden was my sanctuary, it became so much more than just a physical location to me; it became my friend. Or maybe I became my friend. Either way, by tending to my garden, I found a way to slow down, connect to that stillness inside of me, and find the beautiful and perfect soul that resides in each one of us.

As you start to express your own creativity, you'll understand how important it is to live a life of love, clarity, courage, vitality, peace, truth, and possibility. The freedom in creativity is what drives you forward in life—and you'll discover new concepts, insights, and inspiration as you connect with your inner self and your energy source. The act of creating is what will allow you to get in touch with your spiritual self and truly express the music in your heart. Creativity comes from a very deep and pure place; it's about doing things and not worrying about how they turn out. Think of children, who simply express themselves and don't worry about being good enough or having enough talent. The joy is in the creating.

If you start out doing something and don't worry about it being "right" the first time, then you'll allow your creativity to stream through you. This may take practice, as you've probably been trained to color inside the lines in order to conform to society—but after a few messes and practice sessions, you'll start to feel the excitement of tapping into your dreams.

Creativity is vital in a life of meaning because it means movement, expansion, discovery, expression, and renewal. It might not be perfect all the time, but you'll continually be growing, learning, and expressing the essence of what's inside of you. Remember, life is about the journey, and the journey takes participation from you. You'll be able to connect with your beautiful self through an open mind and an open heart. In the process, you'll be able to share your expression, beauty, love, and magic with the world around you. You're able to catch the flow of life and just go with it.

When you plant the seed of renewal in your life, every day is full of possibilities, you're in the zone, you're connected to your inner self, and inspiration comes easily. Ideas and creativity surge through you. It's fun and joyful when you're in the process of creating. There is no right or wrong. You're not trying to make something happen; instead, you are enjoying the process and just having fun creating. You have no limits, and you feel a sense of oneness and freedom with the Universe.

Life is supposed to be exciting and fun. You're here to experience, love, create, and expand by opening your heart. By planting the Seeds of Freedom in your Life Garden, you will tap into your creativity, connect with yourself, and own your life—and that's how you discover the joy of the journey and create a life that matters!

Digging Deeper: Express Yourself

If you want to dig deeper and learn how to renew your life and see the endless possibilities, then you can:

1. Watch the movie *The Shift,* by Dr. Wayne Dyer. This incredible feature-length film is a story of shifting from ambition to meaning; from striving to arriving. This movie—starring Portia de Rossi, Michael DeLuise, and Wayne Dyer as himself—will help you find the joy, peace, and love that you came to the planet to give and receive. It will help you change your thinking so that you can express yourself in a whole new way.

2. Do an art project. Draw. Paint. Make music. Write a poem. Dance. Sew. Decorate. Garden. Craft. Embroider. Build. Bake. Design. Press flowers. Erect a sand castle. Do something creative without any distractions. Get in the flow. See the possibilities. Make mistakes. Anticipate the outcome. Allow yourself the time to get completely immersed in the activity with no distractions, and to just be with your creative expression. What does your project say? How do you feel while you're doing it? How do you feel when it's done? There are no rules or grades—this is your creative expression to the world, so have fun and express yourself!

3. Appreciate your freedom. We live in such an incredible world, and for those of us who live in free countries, we really ought to appreciate the opportunities that we have. When we take the time to be grateful for our liberty, we become freer.

As you go through your day, appreciate all the freedoms you have: the clothes you wear; the car you drive; the food you eat; the things you can say; the money you make; the job you have; the education you've received; everything you can read, study, watch, or listen to; where you live; the person you choose to be with; the right to vote; the ability to come together and discuss matters of religion and politics, as well as opinions; and the opportunity to create, innovate, and see the possibilities in life.

Keep in mind that although we have liberty, we also have re-sponsibility to respect and care for all living things. It's our divine right to be free—yet when we believe that we're connected to all things in the Universe, then we also have the freedom to experi-ence love, joy, and peace in our lives.

Afterword

Notes from the Garden

I've come a long way since I first decided to create my garden. Back then, I had no idea why I was so drawn to this idea or where it would lead me. Before I took on this project, I was leading a life where I was overcommitted, running from activity to activity with no time to rest or reflect. I didn't even have time to make my own coffee!

These days I regularly spend time in my physical garden *and* my Life Garden, participating in activities that I choose to indulge in. I now make my coffee at home (even though it's still Dunkin' Donuts), so I can enjoy it in one of my favorite mugs in the midst of my creation. I sit among my begonias, herbs, and Boston ferns; listen to the gurgle of the fountains, the whimsical music from the chimes, and the sweet songs of the birds; and realize that there are no boundaries between me and the natural world. As I watch the birds, bees, and butterflies enjoy this beautiful creation, I enjoy and appreciate it, too.

Cultivating your Life Garden takes time, and it is not an easy task. You'll be alone much of the time, surrounded only by stillness. Your transformation will take you from a seed with a hard shell into a tender green shoot. Once you break free from that shell, you can soak up the light of love with your leaves, and then convert that light into power and energy for the whole world to see. You'll be forever changed. You'll be free.

I've had my share of trials and tribulations, and I've had to face much of this journey on my own. It took a lot of patience, kindness, and self-love as I went through the growing pains. But the way I'm feeling today is so different from when I started that I have no desire to go back to being the person I was before. I've been reborn as someone who's excited about life and ready to soar into new possibilities. Nothing in my Garden is cause for worry or anxiety or stress. Nothing is trying to outshine anything else; nothing is hoarding all the water, all the food, or all the joy. Nothing in the Garden is worried that it isn't enough.

As I sit here, I'm reminded that for every new beginning, there must be an ending. I may have taken the path less traveled and chosen to live a life in alignment with my highest self and my source energy—but I also chose to end life as I knew it before. The process has taught me that there's always something greater, even if it's unknown.

I am here to be me and live life with an open heart, bring joy to the world, create, and allow others to enjoy their lives as well. We are free when the voice on the inside becomes clearer and truer than the voices or opinions on the outside. I love myself as I am—neither the number on the scale, my marital status, the amount of money in my bank account, nor any other external measure of success determines my happiness. As long as I know that I'm living my life in alignment with my true self, then I am content. I am happy just as I am.

Whenever we seek freedom, we want to be renewed and have a new vision; and we desire to experience peace, love, and joy. In so doing, we may need to fall apart, drop the old, and re-create a new structure. It's impossible to build a sustainable future with the existing structures in our bodies, our communities, our countries, and our world. Yet rather than be upset and resist this change, we can view this shift as part of our natural evolution, as part of a structure leading us toward something much higher—a newer, brighter, freer, and more joyful future state of being. It's up to us to let the old structure die away and create something different. Once we look at the situation differently, then we can see this crisis as an opportunity to find a new life.

If you commit to do the work it takes to care for your Life Garden, then you're well on your way to cultivating a life that matters. You will be flourishing in all areas as you realize your dreams—and you'll be continually renewing, re-creating, and expressing your creative contributions to the world. You will be filled with anticipation about what the day is going to bring, and see all the positive aspects of the world. You will understand that life has seasons and cycles, so even when things aren't manifesting quickly, you know that they're taking root so that they can bloom when they're strong enough. You will know that the quiet periods in life are times of reflection and rest so that you'll have energy and excitement come spring.

How your journey unfolds will always be a divine mystery. There is no way to predict exactly what you're going to experience as you plant the Seeds of Freedom. Yet it's not your job to figure everything out—you don't have to control every aspect of your life. The only thing you need to worry about is tending to your Garden. You've made the decision to give up the old ways of living, and you've chosen to exist in harmony with your energy source. This new way of living is based on being your best self, connecting to consciousness, and seeking harmony in all your relationships.

If you're serious, then you've got to make a commitment to staying on course, no matter what happens or what external pressures you feel from your peers and society. It's only when you make this commitment to live from your heart that you can start to see the Universe work in your favor, helping your Garden flourish and assisting you in experiencing your most authentic life.

Contrary to many other self-help books, *Seeds of Freedom* is about doing internal work so that you can tap into the guidance of your inner knowing and allow your personal journey to unfold naturally. There isn't one set plan for everyone to follow—the timing, the seeds, the experiences, and the number of steps will all be part of your individual Life Garden transformation. You just need to start planting and see what grows best for you.

Take one step at a time, and move toward your joy and authenticity. As you do, then everything else will reveal itself to you naturally—in the same way that plants grow in a garden. When you focus on the present moment and what you need to do right now, you're able to enjoy where you are and where you're going without worrying about it so much. Allowing life to unfold naturally instead of sticking to a specific plan lets you enjoy the magic of synchronicity.

Gardening was something I embarked upon to help me heal. It wasn't about having a hobby; it became a way of life. Today I feel healthy and whole. I'm renewed and filled with joy, but this doesn't mean my life is perfect—there's always work to do and new ground to cultivate. So, I'm on to my next adventure. I'm heading out on a cross-country tour in an RV with my parents and my two shih tzus, Swedie and Cali—I want to discover the sense of freedom in other people's Life Gardens, as well as plant a few new seeds of my own. I'm not sure what my updated Garden is going to look like, but I'm anticipating the exciting adventures that will unfold.

This is an exhilarating time full of new possibilities and expanded dreams. My roots are deep; I know how to take care of my Garden through nourishment, connection, clearing, and balance. I am truly experiencing a life that matters and am amazed by the possibilities that unfold every day. I'm ready for this next chapter.

When new opportunities appear, it's okay to let go of the old. To that end, I left that first garden I planted in the care of individuals who will love it even as they sow seeds of their own, made sure that Cici the cat had someone to look after her, and planted a new garden in a new place with new people. I'm now waiting to see what will grow this season.

I still have the violet that sparked this whole journey for me, but it is now perched proudly on my altar. It doesn't bear any fruit or provide any sustenance; it's there only for the sake of beauty. This little plant has given me loveliness, grace, and exquisiteness, while asking nothing in return.

Violets have become primary symbols of enlightenment for me and continue to remind me of the joys of childhood, as well as the memory of that sad woman trapped in a hermetically sealed office building. Violets remind me of the connection to my higher self, the Universe, and the mystery that lies within the invisible and unknown. They remind me that I can indeed cultivate a life that matters.

Freedom means that our minds, hearts, and spirits are wide open and flowing with the joy of creation. I hope you will join me by planting a flourishing Life Garden of your own!

— Happy gardening!
Heather Wilson
Hilton Head Island, South Carolina

Acknowledgments

Much like planting my garden, writing this book was a journey. Every day something new blossomed or something died; and I just kept tending to the blooms, pulling weeds, removing boulders, and planting new seeds. It was an exciting project, and it has become this beautiful collection of contributions that has been expressed through the sharing of stories. I certainly couldn't have planted such a beautiful garden on my own, and want to give enormous thanks to everyone who contributed:

My publishing team at Hay House: Reid Tracy, Jill Kramer, and Margarete Nielsen for giving me the opportunity to publish a book and share my story with the world.

My editor, Bev West, who used her masterful editing skills to bring the manuscript to life; she is a literary gardener who lovingly helped me shape and nurture something beautiful to share with the world.

The talented and hardworking team at Hay House that includes: Shannon Littrell and Patrick Gabrysiak for their incredible editing, Charles McStravick for the beautiful cover design, Jacqui Clark and Lindsay McGinty for their expertise in publicity, and Gail Gonzales and Heather Tate for their marketing acumen.

To my mentors, teachers, and healers: Dawn, Dr. Khalsa, Jennifer, Maxine, Mike, and Summer. Knowing each one of you changed my life profoundly. Your inspiration, guidance, and encouragement have opened my mind, heart, and spirit to a new way of being.

Those who gave me the gift of support and friendship are too many to mention, but I want to give special thanks to: Carolyn, Catrina, Corinne, Ellen, Gita, Jan, Jessie, Jill, Jo, Kate, Lorikay, Lynnda, Manon, Martha, Maureen, Melissa, Michelle S., Michelle T., Reshma, Runa, and Ted.

Thanks also to the amazing souls in my meditation class for the constant stream of love and support: Adrianna, Becky, Binoti, Douglas, Holley, Jill, Joan, Joseph, Kate, Kathie, Leslie, Marguerite, Nicoletta, Polly, Shiv, and Tejal.

And a very healthy thank-you to all the people and organizations who knowingly or unknowingly supported my journey. Your random acts of kindness, generosity, help, thoughtful words, actions, and invitations have made each step of this path to freedom worthwhile and meaningful. Thank you.

Special thanks to all the people I interviewed for the book and to everyone who completed the survey. Thank you for sharing your stories. This book was shaped and formed into its current state because of the incredibly gifted team at BBDO Atlanta, Joann Sciarrino-Goggel, Annie Hou, Grace Huang, and Xiaona Hu, who helped me create and tabulate the research results for the Freedom Path Study. Thank you for believing in my work and for helping me understand what people believe about freedom.

And finally, I bow in such deep gratitude and appreciation to Summer, for being my spiritual mentor and guide and helping me stay rooted and grounded so I can connect and flow in my own alignment. And to my incredible parents, Howard and Haila, for their trust, love, and support that made it possible for me to write and publish this book. I couldn't have done it without you.

About the Author

Heather Marie Wilson, a 20-year strategy and marketing professional, had an exciting career as the Director of Multichannel Marketing and Director of Credit Marketing for The Home Depot, where she was responsible for a multibillion dollar sales portfolio. She decided to leave the corporate world for a more balanced life that gave her the freedom she desired, so she started her own successful consulting firm to work with companies such as General Electric, Citibank, Coca-Cola, Delta Air Lines, Best Buy, InterContinental Hotels Group, and The Home Depot, helping them with multichannel marketing, branding, and business strategy.

Wilson is now focused on advising and training corporations, businesses, and individuals on how to bring awareness to their personal and professional lives. Her goal is to bring humanity back into business; so she demonstrates the importance of caring for other people and the planet, as well as unleashing the possibilities of life within and without a corporate setting. She wants to help people transform their lives and vocation by giving them the tools, permission, and courage they need to live a life that matters. Her method involves planting the nine Seeds of Freedom that she discovered in her own Life Garden.

Wilson has a B.S. from the University of Massachusetts, Amherst, and an MBA from Goizueta Business School at Emory University. She is based in Atlanta, Georgia; and Hilton Head Island, South Carolina—however, she is currently living a life of freedom and possibility. She's traveling in an RV across North America to help individuals, schools, organizations, and businesses plant their own possibilities and discover the way to freedom. And she plants gardens wherever she goes!

Website: **www.heathermariewilson.com**

Notes

Notes

Notes

Notes

We hope you enjoyed this Hay House book. If you'd
like to receive our online catalog featuring additional
information on Hay House books and products, or if you'd
like to find out more about the Hay Foundation, please contact:

Hay House, Inc., P.O. Box 5100, Carlsbad, CA 92018-5100
(760) 431-7695 or (800) 654-5126
(760) 431-6948 (fax) or (800) 650-5115 (fax)
www.hayhouse.com® • **www.hayfoundation.org**

Published and distributed in Australia by: Hay House Australia Pty. Ltd.,
18/36 Ralph St., Alexandria NSW 2015 • *Phone:* 612-9669-4299
Fax: 612-9669-4144 • www.hayhouse.com.au

Published and distributed in the United Kingdom by:
Hay House UK, Ltd., 292B Kensal Rd., London W10 5BE
Phone: 44-20-8962-1230 • *Fax:* 44-20-8962-1239 • www.hayhouse.co.uk

Published and distributed in the Republic of South Africa by:
Hay House SA (Pty), Ltd., P.O. Box 990, Witkoppen 2068
Phone/Fax: 27-11-467-8904 • www.hayhouse.co.za

Published in India by: Hay House Publishers India,
Muskaan Complex, Plot No. 3, B-2, Vasant Kunj, New Delhi 110 070
Phone: 91-11-4176-1620 • *Fax:* 91-11-4176-1630 • www.hayhouse.co.in

Distributed in Canada by: Raincoast, 9050 Shaughnessy St.,
Vancouver, B.C. V6P 6E5 • *Phone:* (604) 323-7100
Fax: (604) 323-2600 • www.raincoast.com

Take Your Soul on a Vacation

Visit **www.HealYourLife.com®** to regroup, recharge,
and reconnect with your own magnificence.
Featuring blogs, mind-body-spirit news, and
life-changing wisdom from Louise Hay and friends.

Visit **www.HealYourLife.com** today!

Lightning Source UK Ltd.
Milton Keynes UK
UKOW051118070313

207287UK00011B/315/P